INTRODUCTION TO INDIAN RELIGIOUS THOUGHT

INTRODUCTION TO INDIAN RELIGIOUS THOUGHT

by Paul Younger

THE WESTMINSTER PRESS
Philadelphia

ISBN 0-664-20926-2 (cloth)

ISBN 0-664-24944-2 (paper)

LIBRARY OF CONGRESS CATALOG CARD NO. 70-172155

PUBLISHED BY THE WESTMINSTER PRESS ®
PHILADELPHIA, PENNSYLVANIA

PRINTED IN THE UNITED STATES OF AMERICA

CONTENTS

PREFACE

Usually the people who inspire a piece of writing are not conscious of it. That is certainly true in the case of this little book, but I would still like to express my appreciation.

I began writing for some undergraduate students who had fallen in love with India but badly needed guidance if their love was to mature. As with all students they have since passed on, but maybe others like them will come across this book.

As I wrote, I found myself more and more conscious of two saintly older men from whom I have learned much of what I know about the religious life. One was my father, a small-town Presbyterian pastor, from whom I learned to love and fear the divine, and the other, Professor T. R. V. Murti, with whom I was reading Sanskrit texts as I wrote. I suspect that neither will completely agree with what I have written, but I trust they will see within it a bit of that which I have learned from them.

Only toward the end did I become conscious of the kind of people who might read a book such as this. The book, rather immodestly, suggests a new pattern in understanding among people of different religious traditions. It will be only natural that many religious people will disagree with my interpretations. In that sense the book is intended to be provocative, and the measure of its merit will be in its ability to raise anew a discussion on interreligious understanding.

My wife has, as always, served as my best critic and source of encouragement, pointing out both Sanskrit and English phrases that made no sense, but in the end helping me believe there was substance in what was written.

P. Y.

Madras

INTRODUCTION

Is it possible for Westerners to understand the religious life of India? This question is now relevant for thousands who have either traveled to India or in some other way come into contact with Indian religion. Even a superficial acquaintance leaves one with the impression that the religious life of India is fascinating, complex, and mysterious, but, above all, *different* from the religious traditions of the West.

The problem of understanding in its most basic form is the problem of whether one man ever fully understands another. When the men involved have been molded by traditions that have for centuries developed along separate paths, the problem is simply made more complex. The religious traditions that mold men have often been the cause of their misunderstanding one another. These same traditions can also be made the medium through which understanding takes place. The task is to find a way of viewing the religious traditions that will allow them to be media of understanding between men.

The systematic study of the religious traditions of mankind is only about one hundred years old. In the initial stage of the study, the primary attention was focused on developing "histories" of the separate traditions. The ancient texts were translated, the important leaders and events were set in chronological order, and the pattern of development in ritual, doctrine, and organization was established.[1] The second stage in the study of the religious traditions was to isolate the phenomenological structures of the several traditions and set them beside one another, so that common patterns might be discovered. Both of these approaches consciously postponed the questions of meaning and truth. But those questions cannot be postponed indefinitely, and the time has come to take the results of the "history" and "phenomenology" of religions and to proceed to the next step.

The next step, it would seem to me, would be to see the historical and phenomenological materials in terms of the underlying meaning-experience of an individual within each of the several traditions. What do the phenomena that make up this religious tradition add up to, in terms of the individual's experience of meaning? Or what is human life like when viewed through the forms of this religious tradition? This step builds upon the work of "history" and "phenomenology," for it uses the materials these disciplines have set forth, but goes beyond them in reopening the question of meaning and truth.

The question of meaning and truth is opened only in a preliminary way in this step. The distances between men are still respected, and the experience of a man

[1] My contribution to the study of these questions can be found in *The Indian Religious Tradition* (Varanasi: Bharatiya Vidya Prakashan, 1970).

within a given religious tradition is seen as a unique product of that tradition. Nevertheless, the experience of a man within a given tradition does shed rays of light on all human experience. As we examine the experience of a man within the Indian Tradition we will naturally be asking questions about our own experience. How has our tradition prepared us to understand the nature of the human situation, the way men order their lives, or the quest for salvation? Our own insight into experience may be enriched as we gain understanding of the experience of others within their tradition.

This approach to religious understanding should be carefully distinguished from an attempt to construct a theology of all religions. Such an endeavor may someday be possible if in the course of history the religious traditions of mankind are shared to the point where some future generation feels that it is heir to them all. At that time the formulations of theology or the appoaches to truth would all be set forth on the basis of a common tradition and a common experience. But we have not yet arrived at a common tradition and a common experience, and universal theological systems at present must be either missionary enterprises projecting one set of experiences on all men, or abstractions which have nothing to do with concrete religious life.

The religious experience of the Indian is a good one for Western men to become acquainted with. Not only is it very different from Western experience, but it has been preserved in an unbroken history since the earliest times, and it is gradually emerging as the most viable religious alternative to modern Western man. When approached from the outside, the complexity of the Indian Religious Tradition is overwhelming, and yet in the experience of the individual within the Tradition it all fits together. This study will attempt the impossible task of making a digest of the Tradition which the individual Indian experiences available to outsiders. The measure of our success will be, not in whether we have all the details sorted out correctly, but in whether the Indian experience is seen in such a way as to broaden our understanding of human experience.

PART ONE

"ACCEPTANCE"

Indian experience takes place on two levels. Part of it is taken up with "that which is" (*samsāra*),[2] and the other part with "that which might be" (*mokṣa*). A man comes to grips with the reality about him and also seeks the Reality which transcends. His life must somehow combine the "acceptance" which allows him to experience warmth, order, and beauty in the changing scene around him, and the "transcendence" which takes him beyond the changing scene into the liberation to which his life is directed.

This duality in the Indian experience has often been missed by Western scholars. The tendency has usually been to ignore the first part of the experience and thereby to overlook India's sensitive interpretation of

---

[2] The reader should not be frightened by the Sanskrit words that appear in the text. They are not included to make the discussion more technical, but to give the reader a measure of interpretative freedom. None of these Sanskrit terms have exact English equivalents, and I would be unfair to the reader if I limited him to one arbitrary rendering. It is hoped that by including the Sanskrit terms in the discussion the reader will develop his own set of meanings based on the contexts in which he sees the terms appear. The Glossary, at the back of the book, may also be of help.

life in this world. As a result, the West often pictures Indians as inhuman ascetics, when in fact India has been characterized by a warm humanity, an ordered society, and a complex culture. The first part of this study will attempt to describe the "acceptance" of this world which constitutes the first half of Indian experience.

There are four major aspects to the experience of "acceptance." The context of this experience is explained in terms of the concept of *samsāra* (the sea of change). The source or root from which experience arises is the *garbha* (womb). The structure of experience is set forth in the concept of *dharma* (order). And, finally, the product or end of this experience is described as *saṃskṛti* (culture). All four elements are necessary parts of the integral experience that we have described as the "acceptance" of the "world as it is."

1

Samsāra: Sea of Change

The Phenomena

The first question that arises when one begins to investigate the nature of experience is: What is the context in which human experience takes place? Most systems of thought take the answer to this question as a presupposition of the whole system and rarely discuss it. But in a study such as the present one, which attempts to interpret one set of ideas in terms of another, this question cannot be so easily bypassed. When we note that Indian religious thought does not make the familiar Western distinctions between the divine and the human, or between man and nature, we realize that we must go back and ask the basic question as to how Indians view the context of human experiencing.

In early Indian thought there appear to have been two different views about man's environment. The view found in the *Ṛg Veda,* a collection of hymns from before 1,000 B.C., started with the idea of "order" and developed a cosmology in which *devas* (orderly powers) struggled with *asuras* (disruptive powers). Men were conceived of as heroes [3] who participated in the establish-

[3] For a discussion of Ṛg Vedic ideas, see my *The Indian Religious Tradition* (cited above), Ch. 2. See also Chapters 3 and 7 of this text.

ment of order with their sacrifices and hymns. A somewhat different view, found in a variety of other texts, centered around the idea of "vitality" and described the cosmos as a sea of change. In this view, man was part of a mysteriously complex plurality, which swept him along on an unending and incomprehensible path. Although the Ṛg Vedic idea survived, it was the second view which became more and more characteristic of Indian religious thought.

This view of life as a "sea of change" (*samsāra*) has been expressed in Indian art from the earliest times.[4] Even in the Indus Valley civilization of the third millennium B.C., there were a number of figures in dancing poses which convey a sense of the vitality of nature. In the Śunga art of the second century B.C., we find this attitude fully developed. In this art the vines wind through the relief compositions, seemingly bringing the sap of life to a variety of human, divine, and animal figures. In the great relief sculpture of Mahābalipuram dating from the seventh century A.D., the rock cliff is alive with all the orders of life brought together as a background for the "Descent of the Ganges" which symbolizes the flow of the water of life. Finally, one thinks of the miniature paintings of the Rājput period when the gardens of the forest provide the scene in which the god Kṛṣṇa romps with the cowherd girls. These examples, which represent a variety of religious points of view, all seem to agree in setting the background as a scene of plurality and vitality.

---

4 Any standard text on Indian art would contain plates of the art referred to. Especially recommended are B. Rowland, *The Art and Architecture of India* (Penguin Books, Inc., 1953), and S. Kramrisch, *The Art of India* (London: Phaidon Press, Ltd., 1954).

The conscious acceptance of the concept of *samsāra* probably began sometime before the sixth century B.C. In the early Buddhist and Upaniṣadic texts of that period, life is already seen as a sea of change and transience, and the authors are attempting to find the meaning of man's experience against the background provided by *samsāra.* In both the Buddhist and the Upaniṣadic texts, there are hints that, from a very early time, one of the possible interpretations of life seen as *samsāra* was for man to resign himself to his fate (*niyati*) and let the stream of transience carry him where it would. It seems that this possibility was followed out most consistently by a group known as the Ājīvakas. It was also partially reflected in the Jain doctrine that advocates ascetic discipline to curb the activities which disrupt the soul's harmony with the cosmic order. This may be the most obvious response to the idea of *samsāra,* and the one that many Westerners assume Indians must have followed; but it is not the path suggested in Buddhism or the Upaniṣads and has not been followed by the mainstream of the Indian Tradition.

Buddhism took the idea of *samsāra* very seriously. According to the Buddha, all of life was characterized by instability. He was not interested in any theoretical analysis of this situation but pressed home the implications it bore for human experience by talking about the all-pervading presence of old age, disease, and death. The Buddha, at the same time, saw that man possessed a vision which transcended this state. This vision he described in negative language as *nirvāna* (non-changefulness), and pointed out that it was precisely because man possessed this vision that the sea of change or transience confronted him as an experience of pain (*duḥkha*).

In other words, while the context in which man's experience takes place is *samsāra,* his destiny is to find a path to the transcending of *samsāra.* (For a fuller discussion of the Buddhist idea of *nirvāna* see Chapter 7.)

The Upaniṣadic teachers took much the same position as the Buddha, except that they affirmed in more positive terms the transcendent Reality, which they referred to as the Absolute (*Brahman*). While the Upaniṣadic texts do not have many passages that dwell on the painful character of human experience in the sense that the Buddhist texts do, the role of *samsāra* as the scene from which the quest for the Ultimate must begin is much the same in both systems.

After the duality of *samsāra* and the Ultimate was established by early Buddhism and the Upaniṣads, a number of different views were set forth outlining the precise nature of this relationship. The most complex and possibly the earliest view was the dualist view set forth by the Sāṃkhya and Yoga schools of philosophy. (For a discussion of the psychological implications of Sāṃkhya cosmology see Chapter 6.) The Sāṃkhya school posited two realities. The one was *samsāra* (nature), which the Sāṃkhyas called *prakṛti.* The other was the *puruṣa,* the subject or knower of *prakṛti.* The Sāṃkhya school went on to elaborate the evolution of forms which takes place within *prakṛti* in order to bring into being the world as we experience it. This evolution began with the development of the ego and the intelligence and proceeded to unravel as the three forces of *sattva* (light), *rajas* (heat), and *tamas* (mass) gave rise to the senses, the five subtle elements, and finally the five gross elements of earth, water, fire, wind, and space. This version of the structure of *samsāra* is the most detailed and orderly of any in the Indian Tradition and not surprisingly gave rise to the most systematic approach to salvation, that of the *yogin.* (For a discussion of *Yoga* as a "way" to salvation see Chapter 8.) The *yogin* works back up through the scheme of evolution, bringing under control in turn his bodily senses, his mental activity, and finally his highest vision. In the Sāṃkhya-Yoga schools *prakṛti,* or *samsāra,* is never really eliminated, for it provides the ladder through which the *yogin* climbs, and even in the state of quiescence it serves as the mirror in which the *puruṣa* recognizes himself.

The most renowned of Indian philosophical systems, the Advaita Vedānta, takes a somewhat different view of *samsāra.* Advaita Vedānta is a non-dual system that stands for the sole reality of *Brahman.* (For a discussion of *Brahman* as the Absolute see Chapter 7.) The implication of this view, as seen by Śaṇkara, the greatest philosopher of this school, is that the world of *samsāra* is illusory or unreal. The name he gives to the illusory world is *māyā.* The world of *māyā* is important even in Śaṇkara's system, for it is in this context that one has to work out patterns of social behavior and even forms of devotion. But when one finally knows *Brahman,* one realizes that this world is the product of *avidyā* (ignorance) and that the veils in which it had wrapped one's mind were illusory. This position should not be mistaken for either an attitude of indifference or one of otherworldliness. It is, rather, a two-level view of experience and truth, in which it is only through a careful appropriation of the experience of *māyā* on the lower level that one breaks through to the experience of *Brahman,* in which it becomes clear that all else is unreal.

Gradually a third view of *samsāra* became the most

popular one in Indian religion. This is the view of devotional theism, which is found in most of the later art and literature. Basically, this view was a variation of the Advaita view, but it compromised the strict interpretation of *māyā* and said that in a certain secondary sense the world and the soul of the devotee were real.[5] What one experiences in life, and what the artist depicts when he describes the struggle of gods and men is the play (*līlā*) of the Lord (*Īśvara*) in self-manifestation. In practice this means that the devotee can believe that his experiences of joy and ecstasy or fear and abandonment are as real as anything else, or he can find himself caught up in the self of the Lord in such a way that he can see neither himself nor the world as real. While the Sāṃkhya view led to an orderly yogic discipline and the Advaita view led to a rigid intellectual vision, the devotional view tended to depict the mysterious *samsāra* as a forest that combined excitement and color with wonder and awe.

The Implications

Having outlined the Indian view of *samsāra,* we should now attempt to bring out the implications this view has for the nature of human experience. The first set of implications that arise from the concept of *samsāra* are related to the fact that, in this view, the contexts of human experience are vast, mysterious, and unbounded.

5 The different philosophical refinements of this view would make a long list. Among the most important were Rāmānuja (Qualified Non-Dualism); Mādhva (Dualism); Nimbārkar (Dualistic Non-Dualism); Vallabha (Pure Non-Dualism); Kashmir Śaivism (Theistic Advaita); and Śaiva Siddhānta (Theism). For a discussion of the role of different schools in the Tradition, see Chapter 5.

A very conservative account of time is contained in Manu's *Dharmaśāstra.* This important second-century text says that we are part of the Kali Yuga of 1,000 years; that four *yugas* totaling 12,000 years make a *kalpa;* that one thousand *kalpas* or 12,000,000 years make a day of the gods; and so on. Accounts of space are on a similarly gigantic scale. (For a further discussion of Manu's *Dharmaśāstra,* see Chapter 3.)

The Greeks saw the world as a cosmos that was orderly in the sense that they thought there was somehow a correlation between the order of the heavenly bodies and the reason of man. Whether they believed that reason could guide one from nature to super-nature, or that the divine must intervene and add to reason, all within the Greek tradition had some idea of the basic framework in which this meeting was to take place. For the Indian who sees *samsāra* as a sea of change, this kind of order is not present. Man's quest for salvation takes place in the context of countless worlds spread out in space and time. The individual takes form in a long series of unending births, where he finds himself in the company of a variety of beings ranging from angelic spirits to crude awesome powers, all of which become part of his experience of life.

Within the mysterious and unbounded world of *samsāra,* man's natural love of order is turned inward and developed in limited and personal ways. *Yoga,* which is a harnessing of the sensory and mental life of the individual, serves as a means of ordering the psychic life. The rules of family and caste provide a limited social order which serves as an ark in the sea of change, but they make no pretense of being a reflection of the cosmic order in the sense that, for instance, the Greek concept of the "cosmo-politan" did.

The second set of implications that follow from the idea of *samsāra* pertain to the way in which the divine is seen in the world. In the Hebrew conception the creation is the reflection of the divine mind and will. The world is seen as the manifestation of a singular purpose, and it contains a singular goodness and destiny. Because of this singularity, for the Christian all meaning can be summed up in a single symbol, the incarnation of God in Jesus. For the Indian who thinks in the context of *samsāra,* this singularity is unintelligible. Jesus, the incarnate God, reveals, but so does everything else. For the Indian the whole of *samsāra* becomes a veil through which the Absolute is seen. As one walks through the jungle of *samsāra,* there are signs on every side. The early Buddhists, who were fearful of the jungle, marked out a path for the members of their community, but the path gradually became wider and wider until it included all of the jungle. The various gods spin themselves out in a variety of creation myths that light the way to the Absolute beyond. Arguments about the relative merits of various symbols are hardly to the point in this context. All of life is available to symbolize that which is Beyond, and a symbol becomes effective, not because of its inherent truth, but because of its usefulness in conveying the experiencer to the Beyond.

The third and final set of implications that arise from the concept of *samsāra* have to do with the way man responds to his world seen in these terms. *Samsāra* comes to man as the great "given," the reality in the context of which his life is lived. In this sense it is almost neutral. It is neither the raw material out of which he may fashion a great technological destiny, nor is it the domain of an evil power from which one must somehow escape. Neither optimism nor pessimism would be characteristic of the Indian outlook on life, for both ideas depend on the assumption that the world has a single destiny for good or for ill, and the Indian conception makes no such assumption.

The idea of *samsāra* gives men an approach toward their world which is not unlike that of the cautious, skeptical scientist. One assumes that there is much to be learned by watching the patterns within *samsāra,* but one is skeptical about the technological language which says it is possible to "conquer" or "master" nature. India has made major contributions to mathematics, astronomy, medicine, and other sciences, but it has generally chosen to work in harmony with nature rather than try to remake that which it saw as vast and beyond man's full comprehension.

Man's "acceptance" of *samsāra,* however, never leads to the conclusion that this is the ultimate reality. The attitudes of romantic idealism or cynical hedonism that might stem from such a conclusion have found little place in the Indian Tradition. In spite of man's "acceptance" of *samsāra,* he finds that in the final analysis the endless round of births is an experience of pain (*duḥkha*). As a result, *samsāra* is eventually seen as a burden which must be thrown off, a poison which must be extracted, or a dangerous river which must be crossed in order to reach the higher Reality beyond. Although the quest for "transcendence" must become the final goal of all, the reality of *samsāra* cannot be ignored, for it is only in accepting, understanding, and obeying the demands of *samsāra* that the way beyond is opened up.

2
Garbha: The Womb

The Phenomena

The question that arises, once the general context for experience is established, is the question of the origin or source of that experience. The obvious biological answer is "the womb," but in India this is more than a biological answer, for the term *garbha* crops up again and again as a concept that is basic to the Indian view of life.

As far back as the Indus civilization in the third millennium B.C., the art reflects a fascination with fertility and with feminine life. The most numerous objects found in the Indus archaeological sites are the clay mother goddess figurines. These crude little clay figures, which were probably placed on the mantle of each home, are characterized by exaggerated breasts and hips and the swelling abdomen of pregnancy. The other important feminine figure of the Indus civilization is the bronze dancing girl who is nude except for a few bangles and seems to be dancing in what is a lively and almost provocative manner. The clay mother goddesses seem to indicate that this agricultural civilization was concerned with fertility and that they saw a parallel between the fertility of the womb at home and the fertility of the earth, the great mother from whom they received their crops. The dancing girl may be thought to enrich this idea by adding that they were not concerned alone with the produce of the womb, but were also fascinated by the general rhythmic vitality of feminine life.

In the Śunga art of the second century B.C., the clay mother goddesses are no longer seen, but the female principle is present again in the twisting, voluptuous bodies of the Yakṣis (Earth Spirits) who climb among the vines and trees and hang from the corners of the gateways. These figures are part of the decoration on the gateways and railings around the Buddhist mounds known as *stūpas.* The symbolism of these *stūpas* has long puzzled observers who are inclined to doubt the story of the pious Buddhists who insist that they contain relics of the Buddha. In a recent reinterpretation of Indian symbolism entitled *The Golden Germ* (Humanities Press, Inc., 1960), Frederick Bosch argues that the *stūpa* is a symbol of the root or the womb. In his interpretation the lotus plant is the basis of much of Indian symbolism, with the flower exemplifying the life of men, the stem the conveyor of the sap of life, and the rounded shapes, such as the *stūpa,* representing the root, which reaches into the primeval waters and brings forth life. The *stūpa* and the voluptuous Yakṣis, when seen together, become symbols of fertility and femininity very much like those seen thousands of years earlier in the Indus civilization.

When temples were built, beginning in the third century A.D., the sacred inner room was known as the *garbha gṛha,* or the womb in which the spiritual birth of the devotee would take place. The temple developed as a network of soft convex curves surrounding the *garbha gṛha* and, even in its elaborate forms, conveyed the warm earthbound quality that had earlier been associated with the simple *stūpa* mounds of the Buddhists. These same soft curving lines characterized the sculpture that was associated with the temples. One of the dominant characteristics of this sculpture is the large swelling breasts of the female figures, which convey a sense of warm sensuality and motherliness.

The texts of the Indian Tradition are not as warm and earthy or as concerned with femininity as is the art. Nevertheless, they give added depth to the idea that the source of human experience is to be seen in relation to the womb. In the *Ṛg Veda* there is a hymn (X. 121) entitled the *Hiraṇya Garbha* (Golden Womb), in which creation is seen as an emergence of life from a golden womb that floats on the primeval waters. This theme is developed further in the later Purānic literature, where the golden womb theory is again set forth (*Bhāgavata Purāna* III. 20.14), and where the Earth (*Pṛthvī*) is pictured in a number of places as a distressed mother, who must be supported by the gods if she is to bring forth life from the midst of the primeval waters.

Manu's *Dharmaśāstra,* the most important text on the nature of society, uses the golden womb theory as the cosmological basis for its discussion of society. This point is particularly important, for the cosmological discussion at the beginning of this text provides a warm and motherly tone to an otherwise rigid and highly structured view of society. The framework in which Manu sets his discussion makes clear that society is an outgrowth of the womb which supports life only as it floats on the primeval mystery, which he describes as "deep darkness."

As the Indian Tradition became more varied, the

earlier interest in femininity took on more specific forms within the ritual of the community. The consorts of the gods became more prominent, so that Pārvatī, Lakṣmī, Sarasvatī, and Sīta gradually came to have their own distinctive cultic roles. Attempts were made to give some of the gods motherly attributes, so that in some of the sculptures they appear as half male and half female. The cult of Kṛṣṇa in particular emphasized the theme of maternal tenderness. One of the most popular representations of Kṛṣṇa is as the baby in the arms of Yaśodha, his stepmother. And while the emphasis, in the stories of his sporting with the cowherd girls in later life, is on the passion of their love, it is still a soft, feminine theme set in the quiet darkness of the womblike forest. The final culmination of the development of these themes within the ritual was the evolution of a mother goddess cult in Bengal and elsewhere, in which Kālī was the sole presiding deity. The Kālī cult extended the theme of feminine vitality to encompass the whole cosmic cycle by making the "Mother" the goddess of destruction as well as the source of tenderness and fertility.

Finally, there are two other "popular" tendencies in the Tradition which illustrate the meaning attached to the idea of the womb. One of these is the symbolism associated with the cow. While the texts often speak respectfully of the cow, there is no indication that the cow was thought of as a deity or the incarnation of a deity. Clearly, the cow became important because its quiet presence and its role as supplier of milk made it a perfect symbol for the principle of motherhood from which all life springs. As the associations with this symbol became richer, specific restrictions came to be introduced regarding the treatment of the cow, until finally, in the twentieth century, Mahātma Gāndhi made its veneration one of the central tenets of his faith.

Another "popular" way of expressing the theme of motherhood is by referring to the geographical fact of India as *Bhārat Mātā* (Mother India). The subcontinent of India is seen as a product of natural evolution, not a stretch of territory gained within the struggles of history. It is a sacred land because all the people living there are born of that soil (*bhūmi*).[6] To leave that soil is to break with the womb in which one is nourished. In poetic language, this conception of the motherhood of the land of India is often detailed in such a way as to see the Himālaya mountains as the head, the river valleys of the Indus and Ganges as the breasts, the Vindhya mountain range as the hips, and the two southern mountain ranges as the legs.

In art, philosophy, and cultic activity, the warm presence of the womb is represented as one of the most important determinants of Indian experience. While this theme is present in all cultures, it plays a uniquely central role on the Indian experience and is a major factor in determining how the Indian understands his religious life.

The Implications

The maternal quality of the Indian Tradition is clearly one of its most distinctive characteristics. It is not often discussed, because it underlies the whole of the Tradition and is not one of the controversial topics on

---

[6] The ways in which this conception contributed to the social organization and mythology of an agricultural people are taken up in my forthcoming study on *The Political Culture of India*.

which the Tradition was divided. Nevertheless, this maternal quality determines many of the attitudes toward life that are found within the Tradition. In a comparative study like this, it is essential to bring out the implications hidden in these attitudes.

The first set of implications that arise from the emphasis on the maternal character of life have to do with the viewing of life in terms of its natural rhythmic periodicity. Each of the Indian religious systems has attempted to develop patterns of experience that are close to the rhythms of nature. The Buddhist monastic rules are a perfect illustration of this. Contrary to popular belief, the Buddhist monks never engaged in the torturing of their bodies. Their ritual involved a daily round with four periods for sleeping, bathing, begging a meal, and studying or teaching. The Yoga discipline is based on an analysis of nature in twenty-four parts, each of which must be used in bringing about a mastery of the body and a climb to higher stages of experience. The concern for adjusting to the rhythms of nature seen in these formal disciplines is also reflected in the frequently noted preoccupation of the ordinary Indian with the health of the body and the adjustment of the life-style to the natural demands of the body.

The philosophy of life which results from this acceptance of the rhythms of nature is marked by its equanimity. Nature, rather than history, is the background of experience; therefore events are thought to fall into patterns of ebb and flow rather than into a series of crisis moments. Indians are puzzled by Westerners who predict that India is facing a "crisis" and might "collapse." They are puzzled, not because they see no problems, for Indians are very self-critical, but because the concept of "crisis" does not fit with their understanding of the way nature solves its problems.

Much of the stability that has characterized the long history of the Indian Tradition may be explained in terms of this acceptance of the rhythms of nature. Even when there were major changes in the structures and forms of society, it was assumed that the underlying womb from which life springs had remained the same. Its basic rhythm could be felt even in the midst of change. The fact that society was seen, not as a rigid structure opposed to the new, but as a womb from which it could grow, meant that the opposition between the old and the new, which gives rise to revolutionary sentiment, had very little opportunity to develop. Indian history until the Muslim invasions in the tenth century A.D. was marked, not by a series of revolutionary changes, but by a rhythmic flow of political fortunes and a steady growth in cultural forms. Even in the long periods of Muslim and British rule, Indian culture refused to see the "crisis," but, attaching itself closer to the rhythms of the womb, found a way to survive. When in recent years Mrs. Indira Gandhi was chosen as Prime Minister, it seemed only natural to many Indians that their society should have a mother as its prime symbol.

The second set of implications that derive from the maternal character of the Tradition are the uniquely Indian views of the relationship between the individual and his environment. Society as a part of Mother Nature accepts and provides for the individual as a child of its womb. As a result of this arrangement, the individual often feels that the all-pervading presence of the womb makes it difficult for him to discover his individuality. He begins his experience as a part of society and has to grow into his individuality. It is perfectly clear, however, that it is the society which provides a setting for the individual, not the individual who serves society. The warm acceptance of the womb is important in the nurture of the individual, but it never becomes a rigid determinant of his behavior.

The personality type that develops in this environment is characterized by restraint, realism, and individuality. There is no temptation, as in the Greek spirit, to lash out against nature and develop harshly heroic models of manhood. There is no sense of rebellion which could turn one generation against another or even one class against another. Men accept their womblike environment with self-restraint.

The womblike environment, in return, never demands too much of the individual. The mother is realistic about the individual's place in nature and society, so that levels of righteousness and idealism that are not likely to be attained are not set before the individual. In the absence of idealistic goals, there is less of a role for the father image or superego, and the individual is not plagued with guilt for having failed to live up to the ideals set forth. Without the problem of guilt, the themes of "alienation," "forgiveness," and "reconciliation," which are so central to Western religions, are not of major importance in Indian religious thought. It is, however, important to understand that these themes are absent, not because it is thought that the world is perfect and that man has no problems, but because man sees his environment, not in terms of the ambitious demands of the father, but in terms of the accepting womb of the mother.

Finally, the idea of society as maternal produces a

strong sense of individuality. While Western society tends to see the "end" of life as the development of a sense of direction and purpose, the Indian society sees the "end" as the fulfillment of the individual. India has a strong corporate society and the individual is bound to begin within those structures. But the structures play only a supporting role, and ultimately each individual "does his own thing" with the vitality given him through his rootedness in the womb.

The third set of implications that grow out of the maternal character of the Indian Tradition relate to the diversity, color, and variety which this view of life produces. The basic assumption with which this view begins is that the life of man should be as diverse as nature itself. While the Hebrew tradition found it difficult to explain the diversity of languages and concluded that they were God's curse on a sinful people, the Indian Tradition always assumed that diverse groups of men would have diverse languages. This same logic is applied to explain the diversity of social classes, personality types, and religious groups. Nature is made up of this diversity, and those who would argue for social equality, the ideal personality, or the true religion have to develop other bases for their positions.

The "religious tolerance" of India has been seen by many as one of its most distinctive characteristics. Many Westerners have compared this Indian attitude with various forms of liberalism or ecumenicity in the West. This comparison is based on a confusion, for the two attitudes depend upon different assumptions. Liberalism begins with the idea that man in his autonomy determines the nature of his beliefs, and that therefore one man should be tolerant of another man's position. Ecumenicity looks forward to a common understanding of truth, and sees the present variety of beliefs as the partial truths from which the higher truth will come. Indian tolerance is rooted, neither in the autonomy of man nor in a vision of the future, but in an acceptance of the diversity of nature. While nature and its diversity might be considered unreal from the vantage of the final stage of mystic awareness, it is accepted in the beginning as the richly varied environment in which the individual's religious experience takes root.

The importance of diversity, whether it be in social classes, personality types, languages, social customs, or religious ideas, is that it expresses the rich vitality of nature. The womb sends forth the sap of life and a rich tropical garden is produced. Life is not seen as harsh or barren, nor is it made of gray stones that men have painstakingly quarried out of nature's forbidding mass. Nature itself is life, vitality, and color. Man's task is to mature within the warmth of nature and then reach out beyond to find something which transcends this unending flow of life.

3

Dharma: Order

The Phenomenon

Life issuing forth from the womb seems to be a largely undifferentiated stream of vitality, but it is not long before it is formed into patterns that reflect an underlying structure. It is this underlying structural quality in life which will be the focus of our third question regarding the nature of the Indian view of experience.

Even as early as the Indus civilization, it is possible to see the Indian concern for "order" in the regular streets and drains of those well-planned cities. While few cities of that size were to be found during later periods of Indian history, most villages have similarly ordered patterns with central areas for tank and temple and residential areas clustered according to caste. Modern Indian site planning has returned to this orderly pattern with places like Banaras Hindu University, New Delhi, and Chandigarh, all based on elaborate geometrical plans that were carefully carried through.

An important background idea for the later Indian concept of "order" was the Ṛg Vedic concept of *ṛta*. *Ṛta* was understood primarily as a cosmic order that was reflected in the behavior of the planets. It was also seen as a moral order that governed the behavior of the various "powers" in the universe and provided a basis for man's association with those "powers." Man's role in this scheme was to "support" (root: *dhṛ*) the order of the universe through his hymns and his sacrifice.

By the time the self-conscious Tradition was formed in the sixth century B.C. the concept of *ṛta* had faded from the scene and been replaced by the concept of *dharma. Dharma* is from the root *dhr* meaning "to support," and emphasizes the role of man in actively supporting the cosmic and moral order. The term *dharma* is used in so many different contexts that it can easily become confusing. It can mean the principle of eternal order, the good society for which men should strive, the laws governing society, or the moral energy with which an individual relates himself to his universe. Each of these uses implies an underlying principle of "order" which is manifest in different situations in cosmic, social, or individual forms. The term *dharma* refers to order as it is manifest in all these forms.

The basis of the concept of *dharma* is cosmic order. If the cosmos did not have some measure of structure and order, neither society nor the individual would know where they stood. Society is an extension of this cosmic order, in that its boundaries reach into the cosmic realm, and in that its regulations are designed to serve the order of the cosmos. Society is not an autonomous order marked out in terms of the accidents of military conquest or of tribal migrations, but it is an aspect of cosmic patterns and is related to the animal and angelic orders on either side. As a result of its cosmic connections, society is not free to establish regulations which serve its own purposes, but is obliged to order its life in a way which brings order to the larger cosmic framework as well. Society is not the slave of divine purpose, but it is part of a larger order and its behavior should never become an occasion for the disruption of the vegetable, animal, or heavenly realms.

The individual, too, is aware that his life is part of a great cosmic order. He regulates his day according to the movement of the sun. He orders his religious festivals according to the even more intriguing behavior of the moon. And he looks beyond to the stars and planets for guidance before entering into a marriage, a new job, or a new place of residence. In addition to reflecting on the order of the heavenly bodies, the Indian also observes the behavior of the planets and animals around him, and carefully adjusts his life to suit the crops or the cattle from which he gains his livelihood. The individual's *dharma* is derived from Tradition and not primarily from his own observations, but it is always understood as a part of the total cosmic order in the midst of which he finds himself.

The social order, while related to the larger cosmic order, has its own distinctive character and is not an attempt to imitate cosmic patterns. Vigorous attempts to formulate a social *dharma* are evident in the great epics, the *Mahābhārata* and the *Rāmāyana,* which are probably reflections of the thinking current in the early centuries of the Christian era. Even more systematic formulations of these ideas are to be found in the *Dharmaśāstras,* which contain the "rules for society," and in the *Arthaśāstras,* which contain the "rules on politics."

The assumption underlying the attempts to formulate the principle of order on the social level is that the world of *samsāra* is ultimately to be transcended, and that the end of human life is the quest for salvation. In his quest for salvation, man needs society as an ark or platform to protect him against the "deep darkness" of *samsāra.* Society, when seen in terms of *dharma,* is not the reflections of a divine order or purpose. It is, rather, a concrete and realistic structure that will be able to ward off the threatening waves of chaos while at the same time providing a position from which the individual can seek salvation.

Because society serves a specific temporary purpose in the experience of man, its order can be related very closely to its functions. These functions are twofold. On the one hand, it is the function of society to maintain order in the face of chaos. On the other hand, it is the function of society to provide a social ladder by which the individual can move forward to the highest experience of "transcendence." Both purposes have important cosmic implications that form the framework in which they must be fulfilled, but each also demands the creation of realistic and strong social structures. In the Indian understanding of society, the first purpose is fulfilled by the political order and the second by the social order.

The threat of chaos is an integral part of the cosmic cycle. That ever-recurring cycle consists of four ages (*yugas*), each one being worse than the one that preceded it. The present human civilization is part of the fourth, or Kali Yuga, in which righteousness has almost disappeared. In this *yuga,* demons seek power in order to threaten the world, and enemies are present on every side to seize the *artha* (material well-being) of an individual or group. The state is a structure of society designed to deal with the evil of this age.

The epic story of the *Mahābhārata* describes the destruction that raged in North India when the Pāndava brothers were forced to struggle with their cousins, the Kauravas, for their throne. Throughout the epic there are speeches on the nature of government and kingship that call upon the king to rule according to the cosmic and moral order of *dharma*. But the main point of the epic is that the king must effectively wield his *daṇḍa* (scepter of power) if he is to hold his kingdom against enemies within and without.

More systematic than the *Mahābhārata* is the treatise on government (*Arthaśāstra*) associated with the name of Kautilya, which purports to be a work of the third century B.C., but was probably written later. Kautilya sees the function of a king strictly in terms of the maintenance of power and the accumulation of *artha* (well-being) for his people. In order to rule effectively, the king must live according to a rigid personal discipline; but he does this, not so the people will acclaim his righteousness, but so that he can wield the scepter of power wisely and ward off all enemies. He must have ministers who will see to the well-being of all the people for whom the state is responsible, but his major concern is with establishing structures of government which will effectively spy on his enemies, and with developing alliances and a military position which will enable him to defend his domain. The framework in which these realistic views of the role of government are set forth is not that of wild power struggles or of aggressive imperialistic ambition. The framework is rather a systematic assessment of the implications of the cosmic cycle and an attempt to establish a governmental form that will curb the forces of evil and lead to a stable political order.

The second function of society, namely, the provision of a ladder by which the individual moves toward salvation, is fulfilled by the maintenance of a hierarchically arranged social order. The theological definition of man that underlies this system is, not that he is created in the image of God and is entitled to the same rights as other people so created, but that he is a form of the Divine Self (*Ātman*) that is lost in the world of *samsāra* and is gradually moving up out of that world toward the state of transcendence. In this quest for transcendence each man is destined to be reborn in a number of different forms. His movement from form to form is governed by the "law of *karma*," which guarantees a sense of just continuity from one form to the other. As a result of this system, all men find themselves somewhere on the ladder to transcendence, and the bodily form that they possess in this particular incarnation is understood as a reflection of the stage they have reached in the quest. In order to institutionalize this hierarchy of forms into a social order, the system of distinguishing men according to *varṇa* (caste) was established.

The most authoritative statement of caste *dharma* is found in Manu's *Dharmaśāstra,* a work probably of the early Christian era, but built upon a long tradition of social theory. According to Manu the emergence of life out of primeval darkness left the world with four kinds of men. These were not social classes in the usual sense, for a man's position in the hierarchy did not automatically confer upon him either wealth or power. A man's station in life was defined in terms of certain functions he was obliged to perform on behalf of society. The preservation of Tradition was in the hands of the

Brāhmans; the defense of society, in the hands of the Kshatrīyas; production and trade was left to the Vaiśyas; and the service of all was the lot of the Śudras.[7] A man's station in life was important in determining his function in relation to the whole and thus preserving order and stability, but it was more important to him as an indication of where he stood on the ladder to salvation. The hierarchical character of society served the function of outlining a path for men in their quest for salvation.

In this scheme of society, political *dharma* and social *dharma* are distinct but interdependent. While the political structure maintains order, the social structure provides the individual with a pattern of purpose and meaning. While the political order is assigned the negative task of warding off chaos, the social order is assigned the positive task of moving man on toward salvation. The political order without the social order would be hollow and barbarous, but it is equally true that the social order without the political order would not survive the waves of chaos. Each is important to the whole and to the carefully prescribed middle role which society has between the cosmic order and the individual moral order.

Finally, *dharma* is seen not only as a cosmic pattern and a social structure but also as an individual's sense of duty. Most men cannot grasp the cosmic dimension or even concern themselves with questions of social order, but they can perform their duty as taught to them by the Tradition.

---

[7] It is not important for the present discussion whether this picture of society set forth by the Brahmanical tradition was an accurate reflection of India's actual social organization. I discuss that question at length in my forthcoming study on *The Political Culture of India*.

India's most popular religious text, the *Bhagavad Gītā,* wrestles with the problem of translating cosmic and social order into individual duty. (See Chapter 8 for a further discussion of the *Bhagavad Gītā.*) The *Gītā* forms a part of the epic *Mahābhārata,* and the story with which it begins is the scene when the warrior Arjuna is about to go into battle against his cousins, but begins to think about the implications and so hesitates. Kṛṣṇa, who serves as both his charioteer and teacher, argues that as a warrior he has no choice but to do his duty with detachment, since the alternative would be social and cosmic chaos. But Kṛṣṇa also assures his disciple that to do the special duty (*svadharma*) assigned him will be a means to the attainment of salvation.

Manu tried to work out a scheme of individual *dharma* that formulated the pattern in which an individual progressed through life into a path toward the fulfillment of his ultimate destiny. He saw the experience of a man in terms of four stages (*āśramas*). In the first stage a man is a student learning the Tradition; in the second stage, a householder helping order the society; in the third stage, a hermit meditating in the forest; and in the fourth stage, one who has completely departed from society. By providing man with a pattern of development through life, the *āśrama* system gives the "order" in man's life a purpose and direction. When combined with the *varṇa* system, it provides a total *dharma* that at the same time gives a man rootage, an opportunity to fulfill his social obligations, and an impetus to press on to salvation as well.

The cosmic, social, and individual all blend in the concept of *dharma.* At times in Indian history this blend was obscured and one or the other level seemed to dominate. There have been those who ignored social order and individual duty and left all in the hands of "fate" and the heavenly bodies. There were others who allowed either the political or social order to become all-encompassing and oppressive. And there were still others who elaborated on the moral predicaments of the individual to such an extent that his place in a cosmic and social order was lost sight of. But, in the end, *dharma* has remained a balanced concept, and the ordered character of Indian life has generally produced a harmonious unity of the cosmic, social and individual dimensions.

The Implications

The implications of the concept of *dharma* for experience as an Indian understands it are manifold. The most obvious of these implications is that all of man's experience takes place within a universe of meaning that is established and operative quite apart from the subjective interpretation of the experiencer.

The idea of seeing experience in terms of a context of objective meaning was also found in the cultures of ancient China and ancient Greece. In China the cosmic order was the mysterious *tao,* which was too remote to provide a realistic model for behavior and received support from the man-made ethics of the Confucian tradition. In Greece the Idea of the Good was translated into law only with difficulty, and could be fully effective only where the true philosopher-king was to be found. In India the structure of *dharma* was carefully developed in cosmic, social, and individual terms. The cosmic order was spelled out in terms of a social order and an individual ethic, so that every individual was aware of the structure of meaning which surrounded him.

By contrast, the Hebrew view of man did not see the meaning of experience in terms of an objective cosmic order. For the Hebrew, meaning was defined in terms of the subjective interpretation men gave to events as they "saw" the hand of Yahweh in otherwise random happenings. In many ways the "modern" West has continued to interpret the meaning of social and individual behavior in subjective and individualistic terms as if there were no objective standards. The tendency to see experience as a sudden explosion of color and sound that is meaningful only to the experiencer is very different from the structural quality of experience when seen in the light of *dharma.*

The structural quality of experience, when seen in the light of *dharma,* adds a strong masculine tone to Indian life. The warm curvilinear quality of the womb is complemented by a strong vertical dimension. Society is not only loving and accepting, but it has an order, a political structure, and patterns of social discipline. Men feel the warmth and vitality around them, but they also know what their place and duty are at any time. One can speak of the spontaneity and freedom that results from the awareness of the motherliness of society, but this spontaneity and freedom arise, not from an absence of structures, but from the acceptance that one feels within the context of carefully articulated structures. The concept of *dharma* means that the Indian experiences life within a set of structures that provide him with a framework of meaning.

A second implication of the concept of *dharma* is the idea, characteristic of India, that social and political institutions are a temporary ark and are not to be turned into vehicles for salvation. In the Greek tradition, there was a strong utopianism growing out of the hope that the Idea of the Good could, in some limited way, be translated into a political form. The Hebrew and Islamic traditions believed that their particular societies were reflections of the will of God and were to become vehicles of the purpose of God on earth. The Indian understanding did not allow for either utopianism or messianism. Society was seen as a structure that prepared the way for the quest of salvation, but it was not to be confused with the goal itself. *Dharma* was a structure, established in the sea of change, which provided man with a refuge against the threat of chaos; but it was not the end for which life was lived.

Because the social and political orders could not be translated into vehicles for salvation, Indian society generally has been functionally defined. Individuals and groups were provided with functions to perform in relation to the whole, and these functions were redefined in an atmosphere of realistic conservatism. Change was provided for, but ideological reorganizations of society were ruled out as irrelevant intrusions of philosophy into the practical problems of ordering society. The Muslim idea of the brotherhood of man, the Christian doctrine of the equality of man, and the Marxist interpretation of the class struggle all seem to Indians to have certain practical merits; but, as ideologies based on a particular view of the nature of man, they seem a false way of approaching the problem of the social order.

Indian political forms have also been influenced by this careful limiting of their role. By and large, Indian kingdoms have not had imperial ambitions. In contrast to China, for instance, where there was a succession of strong dynasties, Indian rulers were usually satisfied to rule side by side with others. While the separate kingdoms of India could on occasion be identified with a particular philosopher or artist who was patronized by the court, there was no particular religious identity associated with the various kingdoms. The religious wars of Europe had no parallel in India, because the state was not defined in terms of "tribal" loyalty to a single religion, culture, or ideology. In the absence of an ideological identity, the state was seen as a structure for the maintenance of power and was developed in terms of realistic measures to maintain power against both external and internal threats. These political forms may at times seem amoral to outside observers, but they were consciously designed that way. Neither state nor society were to be seen as more than an ark of stability that provided protection against chaos and a platform for the individual's quest of salvation.

A third implication of the concept of *dharma* is that it brings together the cosmic and the personal in the life of man. The individual in the performance of his *dharma* participates in the ordering and upholding of the cosmos. On the one hand, he is preserved from attempts to understand or construct a cosmic pattern of meaning himself, because he is assured by the structures of *dharma* that he naturally participates in such an order. On the other hand, he is not plagued with the possibility that his life is nothing but a round of pettiness that is finally meaningless and of no larger importance. In a society defined in terms of the history of great events and of great figures, much of the individual's concern is in finding if and where he fits into the larger picture. A society organized according to *dharma* does not define life in terms of great events and great figures. Hence each man through the doing of his own *dharma* has a sense of his participation in the whole.

The sense of participation in the whole that the individual derives from the concept of *dharma,* provides a framework for the individual's will to action. Man does not have set before him a series of choices and an opportunity for "success" or "fame" if he comes to the top in the course of his "career." But he does have specific duties set before him, he does have the assurance that the performance of these duties will have cosmic significance, and he knows that doing his duty with detachment will be a source of enlightenment that will lead on to his salvation. While this framework stimulates a kind of activity different from the one established in terms of "success," it is no less a support for strongly willed behavior.

The concept of *dharma* has often been cited as the most pervasive single idea in the Indian Tradition. Taken out of context, it can of course come to mean a variety of different things and is often seen as a rigid social system that all Indian religions accepted. It is, however, best seen not as a rigid social system but as a part of the understanding of this world that adds structure to the warm vitality of life as it emerges out of the primeval waters. Understood in this way, *dharma* defines the cosmic order that gives meaning to man's life, provides a basis for a limited social order, and gives the individual a sense of his participation in the whole of life. Man's "acceptance" of *samsāra* and of the warmth of the womb also involves him in action in accord with the structure of *dharma.*

4
Saṃskṛti: Culture

The Phenomena

In previous chapters I have tried to highlight three different perspectives on life in this world as an Indian experiences it. He thinks of life as set in a vast sea of change known as *samsāra,* he feels the warm, rhythmic vitality of life as it emerges out of the womb (*garbha*), and he attempts to participate in the structures of life as they present themselves in the order of *dharma.* In this chapter we will bring the discussion of the "acceptance" of this life to a close with an analysis of the role of "culture" in man's experience.

The word that I have in mind when I speak of culture is *saṃskṛti. Saṃskṛti* is made up of the preposition *sam* meaning "together" or "refined," and the root *kṛ* meaning "to make" or "to do." It must be seen in contrast to *prakṛti,* which is made up of the preposition *pra,* "before," and the root *kṛ,* and which is usually translated as "nature." *Saṃskṛti* (culture) is a refinement of *prakṛti* (nature). (Following the same analogy, *Prākṛt* is the name for the spoken languages of India and *Saṃskṛt* the name of the refined literary language.) The vitality of the womb and the structures of *dharma* combine to enable man to bring about this development or refinement of *prakṛti*. Part of the Indian acceptance of this life is an acceptance not only of nature as it was but also of nature as it has been refined in man's cultural heritage.

The formula used in the Indian Tradition to define culture is known as the *puruṣārthas*, or the "ends of man." The "ends of man" are usually defined as either three or four. The first three are *dharma* (order), *artha* (wealth), and *kāma* (pleasure). The fourth, which is included in some lists, is *mokṣa* (salvation). Since the fourth "end" is the central subject matter of the second half of the present study, we will confine our discussion of "culture" to the first three of the traditional "ends of man."

The first of the "ends of man" is the now familiar concept of *dharma* (order). In this context, *dharma* refers to the ordered preservation of tradition as the first goal of human culture. In a general way, the preservation of tradition is made possible by the continuity of society, and is therefore a function of *dharma* as social order, which was described in the previous chapter. But the cultural forms of literature and philosophy are specifically charged with the task of continually articulating and refining the tradition and in that sense are the cultural expressions of the goal of *dharma*.

India's literary tradition is founded upon the world's most thorough analysis of the nature and structure of language. The most careful scholarship of ancient India was devoted to the sciences of grammar, phonetics, and etymology. These sciences are seen first in treatises called the *Vedangas*, or "limbs of the Veda," which were developed as early as the second millennium B.C. as aids to the interpretation of the early Vedic texts. Pānini's *Aṣṭādhyayī* in the second century B.C. was the most systematic grammar known to man at that time, but in the Indian context it was only the culmination of a long tradition. The role of these linguistic sciences was to perfect the medium through which the Tradition was preserved, so that a continual refinement of the vision of the Tradition might be made possible.

The most characteristic literary form that developed on this base of technical skill was the *bhāṣya* (commentary). The stream of traditional literature was initiated by a *sūtra* ("strand") in which religious insights were recorded in short enigmatic sentences. A second stage, called the *śāstra,* worked the *sūtra* into a "science" or systematic formulation. In a third stage the *śāstra* received a "commentary" (*bhāṣya*). Finally, a line of commentaries was developed as long as the text in question remained part of the living tradition. The purpose of these commentaries was to reexamine the philosophy of the text, but it was also to develop and refine the medium of language in which ideas were expressed.

Even the literature that is not directly tied to the preservation of the Religious Tradition is marked by a fascination with the science of language. There are extensive examples of epic, lyric, and didactic poetry, but the outstanding literary characteristic of this poetry is an increasing fascination with the formation of ornate images through the juggling of grammatical forms. There are also mythologies, dramas, and histories that are, on the surface, comparable to Greek examples from Homer, Aeschylus, and Thucydides; but in the Indian case these forms are literary adaptations of oral traditions that attempt to refine the Tradition rather than present creative statements about the drama of human experience. Finally, there are treatises on society and government, but they are really classified handbooks that distill a long tradition and do not attempt to present arguments about the basis of moral behavior as did Confucius and Mencius in China, or Plato in Greece. For India, literary skill was a science to be developed for the proper preservation of the Tradition, and in the careful pursuit of that science no other culture has matched India's precision.

The other scientific skill developed as a means of preserving the Tradition was philosophy. Philosophy in India was not the "love of wisdom," but the logical analysis of all possible "points of view" (*darśānas*). The *Veda* had established the basic vision of Reality for the Tradition, but it had left two major problems for Indian thought. The first was the problem of what man could know and by what means. Every *darśāna* presented a list of the "means of knowing" which it accepted, and defended its position with rigorous logic. The second problem was to determine the relative measure of reality that should be accorded respectively to the world of change and plurality on the one hand, and to the world of the unchanging One on the other. Each *darśāna* attempted to present a rigorous delineation of these two dimensions of reality and to establish grounds to explain their interrelations. While there was often a grandeur in the conception of Indian philosophy, it derived primarily from the religious vision and not from the construction of elaborate ontologies. The task of Indian philosophy was the rigorous logical discrimination of the possible "points of view" that might be used as a scaffolding for the already accepted central vision of the Tradition.

Mathematics was developed in India as an extension of these literary and philosophical skills. India has been credited with many of the original discoveries in the number system, and India continues today to produce a disproportionately large number of mathematicians. The reason for this interest is not primarily because of the practical uses of mathematics (although Indian astrologers found mathematics useful), but because mathematics is a deductive science which leads to further and further refinements of a principle in much the same way that grammar and logic do.

The fact that India used these deductive sciences as a means of accomplishing the first "end of man," namely, the preservation of the Tradition, does not mean that they were not appreciated as independent expressions of culture. In many ways, literature, philosophy, and mathematics all underwent a thorough range of development in India and were understood and appreciated as worthy accomplishments of mankind. But in the Indian Tradition, where all of life was worked into a single harmony, these disciplines were seen primarily in terms of their contribution to the preserving of that which was considered valuable.

The second "end of man" according to the traditional scheme was the accumulation of *artha* (wealth). *Artha* was understood in a very straightforward manner as food, housing, social order, and personal security. *Artha* did not have the much narrower connotations that have come to be associated with the term "wealth" when the latter is identified with liquid capital or with the ostentatious expressions of freedom and power generally called "affluence." A person could accumulate *artha* by hoarding money, but he did it more effectively if he produced a family of worthy sons, established his family's "position" in society, contributed to the order of society, or erected a monument of some sort.

The most obvious cultural product of the pursuit of *artha* was the elaborate social network that surrounds the individual. This network begins with the family and involves concentric circles of relatives until one reaches the *gotra* (subcaste), the *jātī* (endogenous marriage group), and finally the *varṇa* (caste). The theory of caste described the system as an objectification of cosmic *dharma*. In practice, caste was an extension of the family that provided a channel through which a man could work for the security and well-being of himself and his heirs. The family-caste arrangement served as a guild which developed and protected the skills of the group. It also provided a system of education for the young and an insurance scheme for the old and disabled. In order to ensure that this arrangement functioned properly, a set of rules for the home, based on the *gṛha śāstras* ("household laws"), were developed as a supplement to the more wide-ranging *dharma śāstras* ("social laws"). These laws ensured, for instance, that the financial obligations in a marriage were properly arranged so that the security and well-being of each family was guaranteed. The proper development of the structures of family and caste were considered a form of wealth; and an investment in them, a proper expression of the pursuit of *artha*.

A very different direction in which the pursuit of *artha* was carried out was in the construction of monuments. The initial form of this tendency can be seen in the sponsoring of sculpture. Many of the ancient art centers record the fact that the work was done in the name of certain donors, many of whom had their own likeness included in the composition. Usually, the larger monuments were sponsored by the king, who sought to express the well-being of his kingdom. When temple architecture began in the fourth century A.D., it was an extension of this tradition on a grander scale. These temples have little to do with the functional need for shelter, for they have a minimum of space inside. Rather, they are extensions of the art of sculpture in a way that met certain religious needs and also expressed the wealth and strength of the medieval kingdoms.

The fact that both the family structure and the monumental art of India were directed to fulfilling the need for *artha* (well-being) meant that these manifestations of culture were carefully channeled along certain lines. This fact did not seem to inhibit individuals from finding expression through these forms, but it did mean that the general patterns that developed could be seen as integrated into the whole of life in terms of the way in which they fulfilled the "end" of *artha.*

The third "end of man" was *kāma* (pleasure). In its narrow sense, *kāma* refers to the erotic pleasures that are mapped out in one of the all-time most popular books on sexual enjoyment known as the *Kāma Sūtra.* The very specific concerns of the *Kāma Sūtra* are a reflection of general interest in the sensuous enjoyment of the world, for the world in which man lives is a manifestation of the sport (*līlā*) of the gods. Man has certain responsibilities in relation to the preservation of *dharma* and the pursuit of *artha,* but beyond these he is free to participate in the "play" of the gods. Essentially, man is still within the garden of creation, and he can taste its fruits and revel in its sensual vitality in an attitude of joyful acceptance. The two cultural forms through which the pursuit of *kāma* is best expressed are music and dance.

In most cultures, music has stayed close to the instinctive life of the people. In some societies the naturally sensuous character of music has been artificially curbed, and music has been used exclusively to express the martial spirit of a people at war, or the transcendental concerns of an aristocratic elite. In India the natural setting was left intact, and music was used to express the whole range of man's instinctive reactions to the world. In folk music the warm rhythms of nature are highlighted, in temple prayers (*bhajans*) the passionate longing for the Lord is articulated, and in the soaring beauty of the classical composition the flight to the higher worlds is set in motion. The *rāgas* which form the underlying structure of this music are patterns of sound that must be woven by the musician in order to reach the underlying spirit (*rasa*) of the art. The artist who is able to accomplish his task produces a sensuous play of sound that becomes for the hearer both a source of pleasure (*kāma*) and an intimation of that which is Beyond.

Dance is both more sensuous and more open to revelatory meaning than the music that accompanies it. Because it is more sensuous, dance has frequently been restricted by puritanical cultures. India, however, has made the dance its basic art form and has based much of its music, drama, and sculpture on the pattern of the dance. Folk dances such as the *Bhangaru* of the Punjab and the *Manipuri* of North-East India present the rhythms of nature in spirited and joyful freedom. The complex discipline of the *Kathakali* of Kerala conveys the mood and temper of epic heroism as it describes the varied life of man in the nine experiences of love, laughter, compassion, terror, fear, valor, repulsion, wonder, and peace.

The classical *Bhārat Nātyam* or Dance of India transforms the sensual into a medium for the expression of the patterns of the divine mythology. When the Indian artist sought to find a form in which the full range of the activity of Śiva, who was the Creator, Destroyer, and Gracious Lord of the universe, could be expressed, they chose to represent him in the dance. Śiva *Naṭarāja,* or Śiva in his dancing form, is the perfect iconographic representation of the cosmic rhythm, and as such it brings to the worshiper a sensuous awareness of the presence of the cosmos in which he in turn is caught up and transformed. The whole of life is a dance, and through the dance the will and instinctive life of man is transformed into worship of the Lord.

Music and dance are cultivated in India as forms through which the sensual is refined and the "end" of pleasure (*kāma*) is realized. Within this framework they are guaranteed a freedom they do not receive in cultures that fear the naturally instinctive life from which they spring. At the same time, the Indian Tradition has enlisted these forms of expression in the service of the whole by making the pursuit of *kāma* one of the ends through which the whole of man's life is given meaning.

The Implications

The uniquely Indian approach to culture is a major factor in determining the nature of the Indian experience of life. One implication of this approach is that the cultural forms express a very broad range of experience. There is no distinction between the sacred and the secular, for all of life is used in an effort to support the central vision of the Tradition. In reference to Western art, there have been those who argued that one should not speak of "Christian art," because such a statement implied a clear line between the sacred and the secular that could not be accurately defined. In Western society, however, it has been generally conceded that a line could be drawn, and theologies of the "church" or of "Heilsgeschichte" have generally been happy to develop this distinction. By not distinguishing the sacred and the profane, India includes all of culture in one interpretation of life and yet also frees culture to go about the task of refining the whole of nature.

The natural base that this arrangement provides for culture also serves as a constant source of renewal and vitality. There is not a single linear direction in the development of an art form or social arrangement. The whole of *samsāra* is available as a source for symbols and fresh springs of vitality, and the culture continually returns to the source for renewed life. While the skills of the sculptor developed in a series of stages during the period when the Buddha image was his central concern, a very different set of skills were picked up when the artists turned to the representation of mythological scenes; and still another set, when they decided to represent Śiva as a bronze dancing figure. In the realm of political thought, Kautilya very early set forth a rigidly authoritarian structure, but the evidence seems to indicate that most Indian kings carefully reexamined the body politic and designed modified governmental forms that were sensitive to the natural inclinations of the people. This process of constant renewal has not only kept India's culture from running dry but has also enabled her to adjust to changing situations.

A second characteristic of the Indian approach to culture was that culture served as a conserving agent. Culture was the refining and preserving of that which was valuable in the natural life of man. While culture (*saṃskṛti*) needed to be constantly renewed at the spring of nature (*prakṛti*), it was able to reach above the natural and pull together patterns of meaning that the experience of men had taught them. The Indian arrangement saw culture as a refinement made on behalf of the entire Tradition and did not encourage creative new experiments, which tend to split the society into those who welcome change and those who oppose it. In the West, art forms often tend to reach into the future with new patterns of meaning that split the generations. Western society has tended to reach out for ever-new frontiers, but has often been less clear about how to handle the colonies acquired or the slave peoples that had been moved from their homeland.

Rabindranath Tagore, India's great poet and philosopher, argued that culture should have a feminine character, for it is the woman that conserves.

> Man took advantage of his comparative freedom from . . . physical and emotional bondage, and marched unencumbered towards his extension of

life's boundaries. In this he has travelled through the perilous path of revolutions and ruins. Time after time his accumulations have been swept away and the current of progress has disappeared at its source. Though the gain has been considerable yet the waste in comparison has been still more enormous, especially when we consider that much of the wealth, when vanished, has taken away the records with it. Through this repeated experience of disasters man has discovered, though he has not fully utilized, the truth, that in all his creations the moral rhythm has to be maintained to save them from destruction; that a mere unlimited augmentation of power does not lead to real progress, and there must be balance of proportion, must be harmony of the structure with its foundation, to indicate a real growth in truth.

This ideal of stability is deeply cherished in woman's nature. She is never in love with merely going on, shooting wanton arrows of curiosity into the heart of darkness. All her forces instinctively work to bring things to some shape of fulness,—for that is the law of life. . . . Woman's function is the passive function of the soil, which not only helps the tree to grow but keeps its growth within limits. The tree must have life's adventure and send up and spread out its branches on all sides, but all its deeper bonds of relation are hidden and held firm in the soil and this helps it to live. (*Personality,* pp. 170–173; London: Macmillan and Co., Ltd., 1917.)

In this beautiful image Tagore expresses the conservative quality that has always characterized India's view of the role of culture. Culture is that which refines and develops the possibilities of nature, but does so in a way that brings together and harmonizes the accomplishments of man, rather than glorifying individual achievement. This view of culture leads to the conquest of fewer frontiers, but it establishes a steady pattern of growth and provides a stable source of enrichment for the experience of man.

Finally, the Indian view of culture leads to a strong element of joyful celebration in life. In one dimension of man's life, experience is to be accepted for what it is. The natural rhythms of the universe are accepted by man as part of his experience. These rhythms are part of the *līlā* (sport) of the gods; and man, through music and dance, which help celebrate the feasts of both the yearly cycle and the life cycle, expresses his joyful acceptance of these rhythms.

Some Western observers such as Albert Schweitzer have characterized Indian philosophy as "life-denying." In the technical sense that Schweitzer used this phrase, it makes some sense, for, as we have shown elsewhere, India did not believe that experience and history were the highest manifestation of the nature of man. But as a description of the Indian attitude toward life, the phrase "life-denying" could not be farther from the truth. As many Western observers who have spent considerable time in India have noted, Indians by and large are a very happy people. They do not approach history with a sense of guilt born of a cosmic Fall and hence do not feel obligated to transform the world as Western man does. Nor do they adopt the Chinese attitude that life is a flat plain of experience where the only meaning is in the moral order man creates. Rather, they accept the mysterious character of life but see it as warm, motherly, and possessed of a meaningful order. Feeling at home in this mystery, their first reaction is to enjoy the rhythmic warmth of their own experience. This is not the Easter joy, which sees the triumph of life over death, nor the eschatological banquet when all the forces of evil are vanquished. It is, rather, the joyful refining of the natural rhythms of the cosmos and a celebration of the natural vitality of man's life.

Conclusions on Part One

The four topics of *samsāra, garbha, dharma,* and *saṃskṛti* are often omitted altogether in Western treatments of Indian religious thought. This is because they do not correspond to the theological questions that have been asked in the West. On the other hand, most serious discussions of human existence among Indians center on these four questions. This difference in emphasis would appear to be more than accidental.

By starting its theology with a formulation of experience, Indian religion gave itself certain strengths and freedoms that other starting points would not have afforded it. Whether these strengths and freedoms will in the long run outweigh any limitations associated with this starting point, we are not yet in a position to know. What might be worth examining is the question of how these strengths and freedoms have helped in the development of the Indian understanding of human experience.

The first advantage of starting theology with a formulation of experience is the openness it lends to the system. One is not restricted to a certain aspect of experience or to an older understanding of experience, but one is free to seek a continual renewal of the religious understanding at the womb or fount of life itself.

By contrast, religious thought based upon a specific revelation is restricted by its very nature to a particular aspect of experience. This restriction extends to every other aspect of the religious system, for the truth is not only accepted in a certain metaphysical form, but it is also identified with a particular community, and almost inevitably with a certain psychological framework. When religious thought begins with experience, it naturally encompasses a wider range and is not, at least initially, concerned with boundaries and limits, but with vitality.

In addition to including all kinds of experience, the openness of an experienced-based theology makes it natural for religious life to accommodate change. Other bases of theology are usually rooted in a formulation which is associated in some way with the past, and the difficulties of finding ways of adjusting to change are usually formidable. Experience, by contrast, is itself a form of change. Not only can it be made to accommodate change reluctantly, but it identifies change itself as the very basis from which religious thought springs.

The openness that the experiential base brings to religious thought also gives it a natural warmth and vitality. The strain of trying for exactitude and the search for sharp lines between truth and error, which characterize much religious thought elsewhere, are absent, for experience-based religious thought bubbles up from a central source and naturally develops in ever-new forms. Calls for "revival" or "renewal" have little place, for the whole religious system is rooted in a naturally vital and living base.

A second advantage of an experience-based theology is its ability to speak to the question of the natural order in human life. The charge that religious thought is irrelevant arises when a scheme of revelation points the way to salvation but gives no interpretation of man's life "as it is." In Western religious thought, an attempt to overcome this difficulty was made with the medieval church's concept of "natural law," but with modern ideas of order shifting to a new basis in "scientific law," efforts to adjust religious thought accordingly have not kept pace.

When religious thought starts from experience, this difficulty is not so great. Experience gives evidence of some kind of harmony between cosmos, society, and man, and it is assumed that laws discovered in nature will have their counterparts in society and individual psychology as well. To assume otherwise is to invite man into a vocation of individually willed actions. While elaborate schemes of "general" and "special" revelations can still build a structure of meaning from such individual acts, the odds are heavily against order and harmony in such a scheme.

When man is seen as naturally in harmony with nature and society, it is possible to view all of life as a meaningful whole. On the other hand, if the religious man's rights over against society, or the society's ultimate destiny as the transformer of nature, are emphasized, the picture of life is one of conflict and disorder. Indian religious thought, by emphasizing the harmony, has interpreted the role of the individual in a way which accepts the meaningfulness of nature and of society. While the individual eventually moves beyond both of these structures, he does so only after they have nourished and provided a context for his understanding of "life as it is."

A third advantage of an experience-based theology is that it provides a framework for cultural purposiveness. The Barthian school in Western theology carried through the restrictive implication of a revelational theology by showing a decided disinterest in a theology of culture. If truth is already known or is to be received only in a certain context, what meaning has the multifarious human quest for meaningful self-expression? Of course no theology disparages human experience altogether; but when religious thought starts with experience, it gives a central place to the refinement of experience in cultural expression, and to the role of culture in the development of the spiritual life.

When all of culture is seen as a refinement of experience, the different cultural forms are less likely to emphasize their own autonomous development. Where this common basis in experience is not evident, it is very likely either that the deductive skills of language, philosophy, and mathematics will burden man with an overly complex tradition; or that the accumulative skills of gathering wealth and power will make him harsh and aggressive; or that the expressive skills of music and dance will make him overly sentimental. India, by insisting on understanding each of these skills as a refinement of experience that contributes to the path to salvation, sought to give them a harmonious balance and a united purpose.

Finally, by bringing the harmony of cultural skills to the service of the path of salvation, a dichtomy between the highest expressions of "life as it is" and the quest for "life as it can be" is avoided. In an experience-based theology, culture is neither a distraction nor an unnecessary luxury. Culture provides structure which is essential to the higher religious path. It provides literary and philosophical forms in which the insights of the sages, which form the content of the Tradition, are preserved; it supplies the material well-being that makes the quest for a higher life possible; and it provides, through its art, intimations of the divine and channels of approach to the world beyond. Culture, understood in this sense, is not only internally harmonious, but is also a purposive vehicle which links the world "as it is" with that which lies beyond.

Man's life can be understood only as it is known through his experience of "life as it is." The context of this life is the "sea of change," but that sea is fully understood only when it is seen to include the warmth of the "womb," the structures of "order," and the refinement of "culture." These four elements in the individual's experience are interdependent and give the individual an experience of this world which is at the same time mysterious, warm, orderly, and refined.

But the individual's experience of the "world as it is" is only a foundation. He is not a disembodied soul, but neither is he a creature satisfied with this world. He "accepts" this world and, in doing so, positively contributes to its warmth, order, and refinement. But in the end he must seek that which is Beyond. Without the "acceptance" of *samsāra,* that quest would not be possible, but with its "acceptance," *samsāra* becomes a foundation upon which the higher quest begins.

PART TWO

"TRANSCENDENCE"

As noted earlier, Indian experience takes place on two levels. The first part of this study is an examination of some aspects of the "acceptance" of life as it is. The second part will deal with the aspects of life which constitute the quest for "transcendence."

The form in which our discussion has been arranged tends to emphasize the difference between these two levels of experience. This emphasis brings out two important points about the Indian Tradition. The Indian Tradition does not see "transcendence" as a natural outgrowth of life in *samsāra*. Neither does it look for the will of the divine to be expressed in the social and cultural orders of this world. The patterns of life in the order of *samsāra* do not lead on to salvation; nor do the patterns of life in the quest for *mokṣa* interfere with the natural ordering of things within this world.

Clearly, there are links which tie the two levels together. The "tradition," which establishes the context of the quest for "transcendence," is an interpretation of the first level of experience which provides direction for the quest beyond. The sages make their interpretation in the light of their vision of the Beyond, but the materials for their interpretation are gathered from the general experience of "acceptance." As a result, man, in his quest for "transcendence," is able to build upon his general experience as he proceeds. The effect of this arrangement is to provide a psychological framework in which almost any element of man's general experience can be transformed into a source of light for the higher path. An acceptance of the womb helps man understand the inner sanctum of the temple where spiritual rebirth takes place. Pursuit of *dharma* with detachment releases him from the bonds of this world and teaches him the meaning of liberation. Expressions of the spirit (*rasa*) in art bring about visions of that which transcends. All of life is open to use in the quest for "transcendence," but only insofar as it is reformulated through the patterns set forth by the sages.

The questions raised on the level of the quest for "transcendence" are roughly parallel to those asked on the level of the "acceptance" of this world. The first question, about the context in which this experience of "transcendence" takes place, involves a discussion of the concept of *veda* ("tradition"). The second question deals with the subjective sources of the quest and involves a discussion of the concept of *ātman* ("self"). The third question is about the objective structures and dimensions of the quest and involves a discussion of *Brahman,* the Absolute. Finally, the question of the end or goal of experience must be discussed in terms of the concept of *mokṣa* (salvation). Again, all four are necessary elements in one integral experience of "transcendence." To know, to realize the self, to be one with *Brahman,* and to gain release are, in the final analysis, a single experience to which all of life is directed.

5
Veda: Tradition

The Phenomenon

The context of man's quest for "transcendence" is the Tradition which he accepts as authoritative and true. In India the Tradition was defined by the sages who had already experienced "transcendence." This meant that individuals within the Tradition were provided with an authoritative guide to follow in their quest. This guide served to mark out the stages in the spiritual life, but it also served as a reinterpretation of the whole of life in a way which made much of man's general experience useful on the spiritual path.

The term used in India to define the religious orientation of man is the term *Veda. Veda* comes from the root *vid* meaning "to know" and can be used of any knowledge that leads to "transcendence." But the term is used in a host of different ways and causes considerable difficulty for the Westerner trying to understand it.[8] The concept

---

[8] Some eminent Western scholars have recently written on the subject. I have reviewed three of these works in the *Journal of the American Academy of Religion*, Vol. XXXVI, No. 1 (1968); L. Renou, *The Destiny of the Veda in India;* J. Gonda, *Change and Continuity in Indian Religion;* and W. Norman Brown, *Man in the Universe.*

of *Veda* presents two major difficulties for the Western mind. One is that there do not appear to be any limits determining what the concept of *Veda* should refer to. The second is that, while the authority of the *Veda* is widely acknowledged, it is difficult to see exactly how that authority functions in guiding the development of the Religious Tradition.

First of all, then, let us ask what the term *Veda* refers to. Any number of interpretations can be found. We will mention only some major ones. One interpretation accepts as *Vedic* only the *Ṛg Veda,* an ancient Aryan collection (*saṃhīta*) of hymns. Other interpretations accept two, three, or four *Saṃhītas.* Many interpreters accept all the Aryan literature from the *Saṃhītas* to the Upaniṣads. Other interpreters focus less on a body of literature and more on a philosophical school, seeing, for instance, the *advaitin* or "non-dual" interpretation of the Upaniṣads as the heart of the *Veda.* Still others use the term Vedic to refer to all of the Tradition except for Buddhism and Jainism. And finally, there are some who use the term *Vedic* to describe all knowledge that leads to "transcendence" and include even Buddhism and Jainism.

The *Veda* cannot be defined in terms of boundaries in the way Western concepts are defined. There are no limits to where the Vedic ends and the non-Vedic begins. *Veda* is like a center of light from which concentric circles of truthfulness radiate outward. Or, to change the imagery, it is like a stream in the center of which flows the pure water from the mountain source, but which also contains much that is somewhat less than pure.

The major distinction that the Indians make within

the concept of *Veda* is the distinction between *śruti* and *smṛti*. *Śruti,* literally "that which is heard," refers to the pure eternal truth heard by the sages "from the ages." *Smṛti,* literally "that which is remembered," refers to the accumulated interpretation of *śruti*. Together they form a continuous stream from the purest source to the murky waters where man stands at any moment. Thinking in terms of bodies of literature, a line is often drawn between the Saṃhītas, Āraṇyakas, Brahmāṇas, and Upaniṣads, which are associated with *śruti,* and the Epics, mythological histories (Purāṇas), and lawbooks, which are associated with *smṛti*. But this kind of distinction is somewhat arbitrary and is not made much of. The purpose of the distinction between *śruti* and *smṛti* is clearly to bring out the transcendent and human elements, both of which are essential parts of the concept of *Veda*. Any definition of *Veda* must include these two elements and see them in a living continuity one with the other.

The second difficulty that Westerners experience with the concept of *Veda* is that, in spite of the acknowledgment of its authority, the content of the *Veda* does not seem to be used very directly in guiding the later development of the Religious Tradition. Hence it is necessary to ask what the function of the *Veda* is in the religious life of India.

The orientation of *Veda* is to the past and the future and not to the present. It does not provide either a sociological or theological test of a man's present "orthodoxy." It is not defined in terms of church structures from which a man can be expelled, or in terms of theological norms from which he might deviate. It is defined rather in terms of a past heritage which provides the context for a man's quest of "transcendence" and a future understanding of the nature of man's highest experience.

The past heritage of man is important as a psychological base and not as a historical record. The accidental events in the life of man are not worth recording, but the wisdom of the sages is essential if man is to be properly oriented to a higher quest. The individual cannot begin his quest by affirming the autonomy of his own will, reason, or emotion, but must begin in the awareness that *Veda* (knowledge) is much greater than himself. In this sense he is accepting a "revelation," but it is a revelation, not in the form of a word from the divine, but in the form of the accumulated wisdom of the ages. As the wisdom of the ages, *Veda* bears a stamp of authority, but its authority derives, not from its strangeness and its association with another world, but from the fact that enlightened sages have stored within it a careful interpretation of all the experience of mankind. Because it bears within it the totality of human experience, *Veda* provides a *context* for the quest of transcendence that is familiar and comforting even while it is authoritative and demanding.

But the function of *Veda* is as much to point to the future as to the past. The knowledge of *Veda* is really the knowledge of the Transcendent, and it is only in this light that it reinterprets the past. The context which *Veda* provides for man's spiritual quest is a dynamic context that thrusts him forward into the highest experience of oneness with the Absolute. *Veda* is not a static definition of present orthodoxy but a moving path along which the individual proceeds to the goal. Within the knowledge of Tradition there is already present an intimation of the highest knowledge to which Tradition points.

Because *Veda* functions in this dynamic past and future perspective, the definition of orthodoxy is similarly fluid. But this fluidity should not be mistaken for indifference. The quest for the pure *Veda* and the necessity of accepting the authority of the *Veda* are essential starting points of the Indian spiritual quest. But both of these are seen as psychological and personal attitudes that can be manifest in many different forms. The repetition of Ṛg Vedic hymns, the performance of Brahmāṇic sacrificial ritual, the exegesis of Upaniṣadic teachings, or obedience to the *guru* (teacher) would all be ways of expressing one's acceptance of Tradition, but one of them alone could not be considered the essential or sole way. It is important to accept the authority of *Veda,* and it is important to strive for the purest expression of *Veda* that one can know; but neither attitude can be properly fulfilled by substituting for them some static and external measures of orthodoxy. *Veda* can be properly understood only when seen as an experiential element in Indian religious life. As such, it establishes the *context* for the quest of "transcendence" and gives the individual a foretaste of the goal toward which he moves.

An active concern with the formulation of *Veda* probably dates from the early centuries of the Christian era when new streams entering the Tradition were seen by some to be polluting the older Tradition to a dangerous level. As a result of the formulations that took place at that time, it is possible to make some general statements about the relative purity or centrality of different elements in the overall Tradition.

The pure center of Vedic orthodoxy is more a theoretical point than an actual sociological group. It comprises the relatively few scholars who chant one of the four Saṃhita texts, who practice the Vedic sacrifice as prescribed in the Brahmāṇas, or who study one of the Upaniṣads. Because few families follow one of these religious paths to the exclusion of all others, pure orthodoxy remains a quest more than an attainment claimed by any group.

Just on the fringes of this orthodox center are the religious practices subsumed under the general title of Vaiṣṇavism. During the early centuries of the Christian era there appear to have been a number of different popular religious movements that were gradually brought together under the name Vaiṣṇavism. Most of these movements were unrelated to the god Viṣṇu to whom a few hymns were addressed in the *Ṛg Veda*. Some of the Vaiṣṇavite literature openly ridicules Vedic sacrifice and Vedic learning and accepts the hymns of the Vaiṣṇava saints as the true religious authority. The great Vaiṣṇava theologians such as Rāmānuja worked Vaiṣṇavism into the main Vedic stream by bringing the Vaiṣṇava literature within the framework of *smṛti* and by reinterpreting Viṣṇu as a manifestation of the absolute (*Brahman*) of the Upaniṣads. Later Vaiṣṇavism has generally seen itself as safely within the Vedic Tradition, even though the popular subcults that center around the heroism of Rāma or the love of Rādha and Kṛṣṇa show no interest whatever in the content of the older Vedic texts.

Śaivism, like Vaiṣṇavism, has remained on the periphery of Vedic orthodoxy. Śaivism has virtually no roots in the Vedic texts themselves except through a few hymns to the mysterious figure of Rudra. There is some reason to believe that historically the worship of Śiva was a central feature of a native Indian tradition that predated the Vedic literature and remained for a long time an alternative to the Tradition as presented in the Vedic texts. On the other hand, Śaivism has an internal coherence in cult and theology that makes it less likely than Vaiṣṇavism to adopt stray religious movements. The great Vedānta theologian, Śaṇkara, who was a major figure in establishing orthodoxy in terms of a rigidly *advaitin* (non-dual) interpretation of the Upaniṣads, was also a devout Śaivite. His reconciliation of Śaivism and what he considered the pure *Veda,* namely, the Upaniṣads, made use of a two-level theory of knowledge. All worship, including that to Śiva, was an activity of the illusory world of *māyā* which would be set aside if one knew the real world of the Absolute, *Brahman.* The later Kashmiri Śaivite theologians accepted Śaṇkara's basic idea that the worship of Śiva could be part of the *advaitin* world view, but instead of working from Vedic texts to their theology, they worked out their theology from their experience of the Lord, Śiva. They saw the Lord, Śiva, in his highest form as the only Reality, who then manifested himself in cosmic and human forms. With this interpretation they thought of Śaivite worship as the true religious expression of *advaita,* and therefore as the height of "orthodoxy" as they understood it. Tamil Śaivites, generally called Śaiva Siddhāntins, have been less inclined to an *advaitin* interpretation of theology and also less concerned with the issue of Vedic orthodoxy.

Somewhat further removed from the orthodox center are the *tantra* and *śakta* sects. These sects center their worship on sexo-yogic disciplines in which female deities play a major role. Historically they seem to have no direct roots in Vedic soil, and have sometimes been described as a late flowering of a distinct non-Vedic tradition. Their own attitude toward the *Veda* is ambiguous, for in some texts they openly defy Vedic authority, while in others they seem to try to fit into the Vedic Tradition. While many of the most orthodox do not like to acknowledge these sects as part of the Tradition, their worship centers around *yoga, mantra* (magic sound), and *śakti,* all of which are ideas that in one way or another are part of the mainstream Tradition.

Most extended arguments about orthodoxy have focused on the special place of Buddhism and Jainism within the Tradition. Among the philosophical schools a distinction arose between those schools which accepted "scripture" as a "means of knowing" and those schools which did not. Of the eight recognized schools, six did accept "scripture" while Buddhism and Jainism did not. The sharpest of the medieval theological debates were between the Buddhists and the Advaitins, and the Advaitins made a great deal of this distinction and used it as a means of trying to force Buddhism outside the Tradition altogether. This charge of "heterodoxy" probably was a major factor in hastening the decline of Buddhism in the late medieval period.

Projecting back from these later developments of the early history of Buddhism, some scholars have pictured Buddhism as a revolt against the authority of Tradition. Such a picture is almost certainly mistaken. The Buddha was critical of some religious theories he had come in contact with, but he never challenged the authority of Tradition as such, and carefully set forth a path which he expected his followers to use in the quest of the Transcendent. There is no evidence that Buddhism ever doubted that a sagely interpretation of the human heritage was the context in which the quest of the Transcendent must begin.

The place of Buddhism and Jainism within the Indian Religious Tradition is unique in a number of ways. Their non-acceptance of the authority of "scripture" meant that they had to develop more direct channels to sagely wisdom. This they did at first by emphasizing the role of their founder-teachers and the line of apostles associated with those teachers, but later on they too developed a body of scripture which contained the words of those teachers. Nevertheless, the more direct link with the sages, and the flexibility provided by a monastic organization that was partially freed from social obligations, made the Buddhist and Jain views of Tradition more dynamic than those of some of the other schools. But it is important to recognize that neither Buddhism nor Jainism reject the idea that the quest for the Transcendent must be rooted in Tradition. They considered themselves part of the Indian Religious Tradition, and most Indians have accepted that interpretation.

Throughout the Indian Tradition, the concept of *Veda* has been used to call the different religious movements toward the pure center and thus to keep the stream of orthodoxy from losing its course altogether. But the main point of the *Veda* was not so much to control the stream, but to provide the individual with a context for the spiritual life. This it did, both by pulling together the varied streams of the human heritage into a coherent whole and by setting forth the path to the ultimate experience of "transcendence." Without the context of *Veda,* the individual's quest would inevitably lack both rootage and direction. With it, he was set on the right course and given strength for the way.

The Implications

The concept of *Veda* ("tradition") provides a context for the Indian religious experience. While there is a great variety in the religious life of India, it is all tied together with an important element of catholicity. Men do not follow their intuition wherever it may lead them. They begin their religious experience with patterns that have been established down through the ages, and they set forth on their quest within the context of those patterns.

The patterns which "tradition" provides for religious experience are defined in broad cultural and psychological categories. There is, consequently, very little demand for cultic or theological conformity. The communities in which ritual is practiced are a network of interlocking groups, none of which demands exclusive loyalty. A man may be the disciple of a local teacher, a worshiper at two or three temples, a member of the Vaiṣṇavite community, and a *Brāhman.* In each group he will participate as he is able, but none will normally demand his exclusive attention. Similarly, in the theological realm, a man may agree with a local teacher's instruction, with theistic devotional language, with a particular Śaivite theological system, and with an overall Vedāntic philosophy. On the level of philosophical discussion these theologies may quite consciously disagree on certain points, but they generally do not expect the kind of consistency in their followers that would be the basis for theological exclusiveness.

What "tradition" does require is consistency with certain cultural and psychological patterns. It is not possible to violate the social norms defined by *dharma* and proceed on the quest for salvation. A man may prematurely set aside the realm of *dharma* when his own discipline and temperament have won him that privilege. But the quest for "transcendence" in a way that does harm to society is a violation of natural law and a false road. Similarly, the quest for "transcendence" may not violate nature by ignoring the basic psychological composition of man. The central task of "tradition" has been to set forth the patterns which man's nature will allow, and those on the quest for "transcendence" are bound to follow in these patterns. It is not possible, for instance, to gain control of the senses by the casual indulgence of one or more of them. It is not possible to gain an awareness of the "self" (*ātman*) by passive membership in a social collectivity. In this broad cultural and psychological sense, the Indian Tradition provides an authority for the individual's religious life. It is not rigid about specific cultic and theological loyalties, but neither does it leave the individual on his own. It attempts to provide a context of meaning for both his collective and individual experience in such a way that he finds himself on an already established path, even though he treads it alone.

In attempting to provide the individual with an interpretation of the collective experience of man, the concept of *Veda* ("tradition") becomes the key to the Indian view of history. The concept of *Veda* interprets man's experience as a living stream that manifests the highest Reality. In some ways this idea might be compared to

Hegel's attempt to give a historical dimension to Idealism. The problem is not the same, in that the Real of Indian Absolutism is not established by reason, but is known through the "tradition," which passes along a trans-rational vision. For the Indian, the Real is manifest in men's experience because it is in the higher levels of that experience that Truth can be known. Truth is defined in experiential rather than rational terms, and therefore the Idealist's contrast between the world of ideas or philosophy and the world of experience or history is not accepted as such. History is the manifestation of the Real, but only in the special sense that the whole of man's experience is seen in the light of the highest experience of the sages. Man cannot redefine Truth through his action in history, but he can come to know Truth through the collective experience of mankind.

The interpretation of the collective experience of man that this view of history requires is said to come from the *ṛṣis* (sages). This interpretation is not made by man because the *Veda* that is heard by the *ṛṣis,* while embodied in their experience, reaches back beyond the "ages." Indians object to the Hebrew view of history because it involves the imposition of an arbitrary will which interferes with the ordinary course of nature. Yet the Indian view is like the Hebrew view where it interprets the collectivity of human experience in terms of a pattern of meaning which transcends that experience itself. The terms "revelation" and "history" have taken on specifically Hebrew connotations in much Western usage, but if they are used in a broader sense, one could describe the *Veda* as the "revelation" of Truth in "history." The Indian interpretation of history does not involve a willful altering of the destiny of a special people, but it does involve seeing a higher meaning in the course of human experience than is available by natural observation.

If there is meaning in human experience, does it follow that history is moving forward or that there is a final purpose to human life? It has been generally thought that the Indian view of life did not support a sense of purpose or progress. This notion is based on the fact that the Indian sees human life set against a background of cosmic cycles in which life appears, only to disappear again. Over against this cyclical background is the element of hope which pervades all of Indian life. This hope is rooted in two basic assumptions. One is the assumption that salvation (*mokṣa*) is possible, so that there is no need for despair no matter how long and arduous the road. The second assumption is that man's problems are rooted in ignorance (*avidyā*) rather than in evil, and therefore time is on the side of the enlightener, the *Veda*. The cosmic cycle itself is not hopeful, but *Veda* ("tradition") is a force running counter to the cosmic cycle, and eventually it will draw men up beyond the cosmic rhythms to the meaning that transcends.

Finally, the concept of *Veda* ("tradition") enables the individual to give meaning to his varied experiences. Because it is designed to give meaning to experience, the *Veda* was expressed in psychological language. This experiential and psychological language avoided the dichotomy between ontological and sociological language which has been characteristic of the West. As a result, questions of truth and behavior are never separated, and there is no pendulum swing from ontological statements that have no relevance to experience, to behavioristic statements that are unable to talk about the meaning of life. When tradition is defined in terms of ontology, it leads to increasingly rigid doctrinal orthodoxy that has no relation to experience. When tradition is defined sociologically, individuals become committed to social forms which outlive their usefulness and cannot be justified as providing meaning for human life. The *Veda* sets forth patterns that are living and experiential, and raises these patterns into a structure of meaning that relates man's experience to the highest Reality.

The highest product of *Veda* is not a full system of theology or a conservative society, but the dawning of "wisdom" (*jñāna*). Wisdom is the synthesis of experience that puts together the pieces in a way that reveals a higher light. The man who experiences *jñāna* has already been led by the *Veda* to the Truth which is Beyond. He has discovered in his self-understanding the Reality which is beyond him and beyond the world of *samsāra*. This discovery is in turn seen to be the salvation (*mokṣa*) to which the whole of life is directed. "Tradition" (*Veda*) is thus not a cultural product that in a detached way provides a context for the salvation quest of man, but it is the living body in which the patterns of his life are molded and the dawning of the sacred *jñāna* (wisdom) takes place.

6
Ātman: Self

The Phenomena

The quest for salvation begins with the discovery of the self. This quest represents the natural development of the individual who lives in the context of "tradition." The quest begins with a longing for rootedness and depth, and in its initial stages, at least, has an ordered feminine character that looks modestly and carefully within.

In the Upaniṣads and early Buddhism the "self" is defined in very experiential terms. The favorite Upaniṣadic image speaks of the "self" as that which underlies the sheaths of experience, namely, the *anna* (body), *prāna* (breath), *manas* (mind), *vijñāna* (consciousness), and *ānanda* (bliss). Another Upaniṣadic image speaks of the "self" as the level of experience beyond "deep sleep," which in turn is beyond "dreamy sleep" and "wakefulness." In these images, *ātman* ("self") is beyond ordinary experience and yet constitutes the reference point from which all experience take its meaning.

The Buddhist texts from the same period use some of the same images, but press further the implications of the mystery underlying experience. When the young prince Gautāma asked about the experiences of disease, old age, death, and the pain produced by ascetic discipline, he discovered that the essence underlying these experiences was nothing but transience (*anitya*) itself. In order to emphasize this transient character of man's deepest experience, the Buddhists went on to describe it as *anātman* or soullessness.

While the Buddhists describe this underlying mystery as *anātman* and the Upaniṣadic teachers describe it as *ātman,* they are agreed in seeing this dimension of experience as the source of man's religious life and the stimulus for the quest for "transcendence." Both interpretations agree that the final existential statement that can be made about experience is that it is pain (*duḥkha*). The concept of *duḥkha* indicates that man's deepest experience contains a vision of that which "transcends" even while he bears the marks of transience. With the concept of *duḥkha* establishing the direction of the quest, later schools went back to reexamine the concept of "self" (*ātman*) in order to find structures through which the quest could be pursued.

The schools of Indian thought that became prominent in the latter part of the pre-Christian era were primarily concerned with analyses of the "self" that would provide a breakdown of the stages in the quest for "transcendence." The best-known among these schools was the Sāṃkhya school, which also provided the philosophical basis for the Yoga school's stages on the way to "transcendence." (For a further discussion of the Sāṃkhya school, see Chapter 1.) The Sāṃkhya school saw a duality in experience between subject and object. Extending this idea, they saw Reality as a duality of *puruṣa* (subject or self) and of *prakṛti* (object or nature). In this analysis, *puruṣa* is the passive observer which stimulates the evolution of *prakṛti*. The three forces in this evolution are light, heat, and mass, and when their original harmony is disturbed, a world of constantly evolving patterns is created. In the Yoga school, these evolving patterns are arranged in such a way as to form a hierarchy of experiences. The *yogin* moves up through this hierarchy by first yoking the senses which experience the gross elements, then in turn the breathing and mental processes, until he brings the evolution of *prakṛti* to a halt. The "self" in these schools is the passive subject which is "released" when the activity of *prakṛti* is brought under control.

The Abhidharma school of Buddhism represents a variation on this system. This Buddhist school accepts the network of evolving patterns but rejects the dualistic framework which surrounds it in the Sāṃkhya. For the Abhidharma Buddhists the evolving patterns (which they call *dharmas*) are the sole reality. The discipline of the monk is designed to bring about the quieting of the flux of the evolving patterns by following the way of the Buddha to a state where "change" is transcended. In this system, as in the Sāṃkhya-Yoga, the true "self" is distinct from the empirical self, which as a part of the scene of flux disappears with the quieting of the *dharmas*. While the earlier teachers had seen the "self" as a mysterious dimension out of which the quest for "transcendence" was born, these "realistic" schools used the analysis of the "self's" experience to construct a path along which to pursue that quest.

By the second century of the Christian era a third approach to the understanding of the "self" was beginning to emerge. The approach of the Sāṃkhya and Abhidharma schools had led to an ever increasing network of entities and an ever more complex pattern of discipline, but it had also taken the element of mystery out of the idea of the "self." The Buddhist philosopher Nāgārjuna set forth a critique of the realistic approach to reality which undercut the position of these schools. Essentially, his point was that one should not attribute reality to transient entities, for they are "dependent" and have no *svabhāva* (independent reality) of their own. Each claim to interpret reality from the perspective of the transient world proves to be void, and it becomes necessary to see truth on a higher plane as The Void (*Śūnya*). Having arrived at this higher plane through the dialectical rejection of other views, Nāgārjuna does not go on to define the "self" from this perspective. Later Buddhist schools reasoned that only consciousness could record the dialectical rejection of the realistic views of reality, and they therefore identified *Śūnya* with *Prajñā* (Transcendental Wisdom) and made consciousness (*vijñāna*) the essence of the "self."

For the orthodox schools, too, the dialectic of Nāgārjuna had made it impossible to continue defining the "self" in terms of the experience of the transient world. Śaṇkara and others went back to the Upaniṣadic texts looking for clues and rediscovered the mysterious quality in the "self" by defining it as the mirror image of the Transcendent (*Brahman*). *Ātman* was seen as identical with *Brahman* and the experience of individuality and the empirical self was set aside as illusory. In this view an awareness of the "self" was not built up by means of a climb through the forms of this world, but by means of a transcendental vision (*jñāna*) which revealed the *ātman* ("self") as already identical with the goal (*Brahman*).

In the later religious practice of India, the starkly transcendental view of the "self" that resulted from the critique of Nāgārjuna and the position of Śaṇkara had to undergo considerable modification. The devotional schools never denied the proposition that the "self" was identical with *Brahman,* but they referred constantly to "selves" in individualistic terms. These "selves" are described as the "lovers" or the "cattle" whose devotion the Lord cherishes as part of his "sport." The schools of sexo-yogic (*tantric*) practice also in theory accepted the idea of the "self" as identical with *Brahman,* but, in the development of the "self" to its highest attainments, they encouraged a highly emotional and assertive view of the "self."

The warmth and vitality contained in these later views of the "self" should be seen, not as a departure from earlier ideas, but as their final fulfillment. These later images still contain the sense of the mysterious quest that resulted from the Upaniṣadic and early Buddhist analysis of the "self" of experience. They also contain all the evolving patterns that the rational analysis of the Sāṃkhya and Abhidharma schools used in outlining the activity of the "self." And finally, they assume the perspective which says that the individual "self" is unreal except as it appears as a manifestation of the divine sport. All of these interpretations can be woven together in the individual's experience of the "self" as the *source* of the higher quest. It is in developing an awareness of the "self" that gives rootage and life to this quest that the Indian Tradition is in agreement. Most views of the "self" in some measure combine the elements of mystery, structure, and warmth, but their truthfulness lies in their ability to reveal the "self" as an intimation of that which transcends, and, as a source of life for the higher quest.

The Implications

The first implication of the doctrine of the "self" in Indian religious thought is that it makes clear that the quest for "transcendence" arises in the midst of life through the asking of existential questions. The Buddha began by asking about the universal experiences of old age, disease, and death. The Upaniṣads attempted to find the principles underlying life and death, consciousness and bliss. The Indian Tradition never allowed the quest for salvation to become a remote theoretical possibility that man could turn to when his practical sciences could take him no farther. The quest for salvation was the natural expression of the life of the "self." Every experience of the "self" raised the question of man's being, and he could not proceed until the nature of man's existence was faced.

The existential character of the Indian religious quest has stimulated two somewhat different kinds of criticism. The first is that this kind of existentialism leads too quickly to the ontological question and provides no basis for morals or ethics. We have an elaborate analysis of the nature of man, but it does not conclude with a very clear picture of what man should do. The difficulty with this critique is that it oversimplifies the problem of the bases that underlie human behavior. Where religious practice is a matter of obeying the expressed will of God, as it is in Judaism and Islam, it is possible to define how man should behave and then continue to refine it. But where religion is primarily a matter of entering a relationship of some sort with God, human behavior patterns serve only as a preparation for, or a subsequent reflection of that relationship. When the apostle Paul defined Christianity in terms of a relationship with God, he was accused of abandoning the law and providing too little guidance for human behavior. Puritan Christianity made up for this lack by combining the Hebrew system of law with the idea that behavior according to that law was an evidence of the grace of God already received. In the Indian understanding, the importance of the "self's" relationship with the Transcendent precluded the possibility of the concerns of morality overriding the concerns of religion in this way. In the Indian arrangement, *dharma* was provided to regulate human behavior prior to the quest for salvation, and conceptions such as *jīvanmukta* (Vedāntic) and *bodhisattva* (Buddhist) were provided to channel the activity of one who had already been enlightened. But these guides to behavior were always secondary, and they never set aside the existential question of the nature of human existence. (For a further discussion of these ideas, see Chapter 8.)

The second critique of the existential character of the Indian concept of "self" suggests that this concept makes the quest for salvation a humanistic enterprise. The argument is that this quest is part of natural evolution, for it does not involve the revelation of a being outside of the "self." This critique represents either a basic misunderstanding of the Indian system or a very narrow view of the meaning of revelation. It is true that India did not think of "Transcendence" in terms of the invasion of this world by an alien spirit, but neither did it think of the quest for salvation as a natural product of life in *samsāra.* The questions about the mystery of human existence arise precisely because the "self" is not at home in the world. The quest for salvation begins as an existential longing of the "self," but the existential longing is born not of human self-satisfaction but of intimations of the Transcendent that are present deep within the "self" of man. The existential question regarding man's ordinary experience gives rise to the awareness of the "self," but it by no means limits its ultimate depth. The conception of "self" arises in the midst of life, but it goes on to develop a complexity and mystery which take man far beyond the "natural" (*samsāra*) confines in which his self-awareness was born.

The second implication of the doctrine of the "self" is that the "self" is complex. Probably no other tradition had as elaborate a view of the nature of man. Man is a microcosm in himself. He contains all the elements that make up the world as well as a series of spiritual levels that contain in various measures the divine life itself.

The life of man in its profoundest levels is a reflection of the whole life of the universe. The cosmic myths are all relived within the life of the individual, and the medieval accounts of these myths slip back and forth between cosmic and personal language. The depth psychology schools of Freud and Jung have discovered in Western man a dimension of life that has always been taken for granted in the Indian Tradition. From this perspective individuals are seen in terms of classic "types," but are also accepted by their immediate family with profound respect for their individuality. Individuals are analyzed in terms of the balance of *sattva* (light), *rajas (*heat), and *tamas* (mass) that they possess, and names are often given in an attempt to identify the "type" of personality. This naming process can become quite complex and not only involves names of mythic heroes such as Kṛṣṇa or Sīta, but concepts such as Prakāṣa (light) or Gītā (song), and even complex theological doctrines such as Bhaktivedānta (devotional nonduality) or Vivekānanda (discriminating bliss). This interest in the depths underlying the personality does not lead to a bypassing of a person's individuality, but rather enriches the nature of individuality as it gives him the opportunity to fulfill his deepest self.

The complexity of the conception of the "self" also affects the way in which the path to salvation is understood. In some Western theology, "faith" is seen as a flash of fire which either ignites or does not. In the Indian conception, the complex structures of the "self" become the steps in the development of "faith." This is most evident in *Yoga* where the path to salvation centers almost exclusively around this disciplined development, but it is characteristic of all paths to salvation in some measure. To use a Pauline image, the "spirit groaneth within" as it carries man forward to union with the Supreme Spirit. Salvation in this perspective is never seen as the quick flash that is often characteristic of religious thought in China, Japan, and some Western systems. Salvation may emphasize the discipline of *Yoga,* the grace of the Lord, or the knowing of the Transcendent (*Brahman*), but in each case the process of salvation is an elaborate transformation of the "self." This emphasis on the process of salvation through the complex structures of the "self" lends an orderly and rational character to Indian religious life. Vigorous activity, warm emotion, and mystical vision are all to be found on the spiritual path, but not their counterparts of violence, wild passion, and other worldly self-abandonment. Whatever the means, salvation consists in a transformation of the "self" and the development of the higher life out of the "self" that our experience has already discovered.

The third notable characteristic of the "self" as the Indian Tradition has understood it, is that it possesses the mystery of Reality within itself. There are hints of this kind of thought within the Biblical account of creation when man is made in the "image of God." This idea is never made much of in the Hebrew tradition because sin immediately enters the picture and the question becomes whether man has any relationship with God at all. In the Indian account alienation because of sin and guilt were not the problem. Therefore, the kind of polar relationship that is described by Martin Buber as an I-Thou relationship has very little appeal. Man's problem is not alienation, but ignorance (*avidyā*) of the truest dimensions of his "self."

Man is on the divine side of the problem of understanding. It is not man and the world over against God, but the Supreme Self and the human self as knowing subjects that become immersed in the world of manifold forms. For practical purposes, the human self is often lost among these forms. But he will never be "discovered" there by experimentation. He is not a superior "form," but a knowing "subject." The possibility of interpreting man behavioristically is totally absurd to the Indian. Man's selfhood is not the product of his responses to the experiences of *samsāra*. Selfhood is the life of the Supreme within the forms of *samsāra,* and it is the release from those forms which is the ultimate end of its life.

The "self" of man from beginning to end constitutes a special dimension of life. A man does not become a "self" when he is reborn into a higher life, but he is a "self" in the whole of his life as a subject. The presence of this "self" in the life of man necessitates that life be a quest and also constitutes the pattern along which that quest is to proceed. The presence of the Supreme in the "self" makes much of life seem a burden of pain (*duḥkha*), but it also provides a mysterious beauty to what might otherwise be so plain. The "self" in man constitutes the source of his spiritual quest and also provides him with an intimation of the nature of that which transcends.

7

Brahman: The Transcendent

The Phenomena

With the discovery of the "self" (*ātman*), the individual finds that he is caught up in an experience which transcends the world of *samsāra.* He discovers that he lives in the shadow of the Real; so that the quest for the "self" is transformed into the quest for the Transcendent, and the reality of the world around begins to fade from view.

The images of the Transcendent that arise in the Tradition are as diverse as the Tradition itself. The structure of the Tradition is such that the highest Reality is not made manifest in a specific revelation, but is known in symbols that arise out of the experience of man. Thus in every image there is a balance between the highest Absolute and the form in which the Absolute is expressed. At times one or the other predominates, but neither is ever found without some awareness of the other.

In the hymns of the *Ṛg Veda,* it is the activity of the "powers" known as the *asuras* (awesome) and *devas* (beneficent) that is most evident. But these "powers" operate under the overarching principle of order known as *ṛta.* The poet or sage who sets forth his vision (*dhī*) in the hymn and the sacrifice, uses the "powers" as he attempts to reach out and participate in the order of *ṛta.* In these hymns the otherness of the Transcendent is emphasized, and the vision through which man reaches out to the divine is a vigorous masculine adventure into the vast unknown.

The Upaniṣadic view of the Transcendent was expressed in the concept of *Brahman.* The etymology of this term is not clear. Some interpreters feel it comes from a root meaning "power" or "strength" with a cosmic connotation, while others feel that it is rooted in the idea of "prayer" or "ritual." In the context of the Upaniṣadic teachings, *Brahman* refers to the Absolute which is beyond attribution. It is *neti neti* (not this, not that). It is the principle behind the light in the sun and all the powers of the cosmos. But it is known principally as the ultimate point in the spiritual path. The teacher leads the pupil along the path until in a visionary awareness he knows (*jñāna*) *Brahman,* and all else becomes unreal.

The early Buddhist view of the Transcendent is similar to the Upaniṣadic view, but differs in a number of important ways. The Buddhists were fearful that the Transcendent quality of the visionary goal would be compromised if any affirmative statements were made. Therefore they spoke of the Transcendent in the negative language of *Nirvāna* (non-breath). Their favorite image for *Nirvāna* was the image of the "other shore" which was reached after the "crossing" of the stream. Because of their suspicion of metaphysical language, the vehicle for crossing the stream was described in psychological language as a series of eight steps which constitute a raft on which one floats away from "this shore." Adrift in the center of the stream, one enters the unknown, and then finally reaches the "other shore," which is beyond all description.

The later schools of Buddhism attempted to develop this approach to the idea of transcendence in a number of different ways. The monastic schools of what has been called "southern" Buddhism took the idea that *Nirvāna* could not be described to mean that no metaphysical discussions were allowed, and they therefore concentrated their energies on defining the "path" through which one gains releases from pain. Because these schools made no positive statements about the Transcendent and did not set forth a metaphysical system to support their view of the Transcendent, they have sometimes been mistakenly labeled "atheists." It may be possible to argue that they were non-theists in terms of some specific metaphysical system of theism, but their acceptance of the Transcendent is clearly attested to by their attempt to get beyond the world of *samsāra.* The experience of *duḥkha* (pain) was never thought of as an imperfection within life, but as a conclusion about the whole of life when seen in the light of the Transcendent. Even the Buddhist monks who concentrated on the details of the "path" were keenly aware of the Transcendent to which the "path" was a pointer. Their metaphysical skepticism should not be allowed to obscure this basic religious posture.

Nāgārjuna, a second-century Buddhist philosopher (also discussed in Chapter 6), felt that the monks of "southern" Buddhism had been inconsistent in not extending their metaphysical skepticism to include a skepticism about the reality of the transient *dharmas.* Nāgārjuna concluded that no reality could be said to be *svabhāva* (self-sustaining) and that all was "relative." Reason, through the dialectic, could demonstrate the relativity of all reality, but it also thereby demonstrated the limits of reason and the necessity of a higher realm beyond this relativity. As a dimension in the dialectic, Nāgārjuna labeled this realm *Śūnya* (the Void). In the context of religious experience he was willing to speak of it as the *Tathāgata,* the Buddha as the Highest Reality; *Prajñā,* the Highest Wisdom; or *Nirvāna,* the Transcendent. Because the Transcendent in this view is not seen as a theistic being in polar relationship with man, it is possible to think of the *Tathāgata* as both an Ultimate that is beyond divinity, and the all-enveloping Reality that pervades all of life. (Compare Eckhart's "Godhood" and Tillich's "Ground of Being.")

The "northern" Buddhist schools, which accepted the dialectic of Nāgārjuna, tried to balance the remoteness of the Transcendent as Nāgārjuna had conceived it with a number of more intimate images. For some, the *Tathāgata* was identified with the historical personage of the Buddha in order to provide a form of the Transcendent that could be worshiped. This conception was formulated in the doctrine of the *Trikāya,* (Three Bodies of the Buddha). The *Dharmakāya* represented the Buddha as the Highest Reality; the *Saṃbhogakāya,* the Buddha as a Cosmic Principle; and the *Nirmānakāya,* the Buddha as he appears in history in changing forms. Once this set of imagery was adopted, it was possible to think of the Buddha in a variety of ways, both within the cosmos and within the experience of the individual, without really compromising his ultimate transcendent reality.

The most interesting development of this imagery from the point of view of the religious experience was the development of the conception of the *bodhisattva.* The *bodhisattva* was thought of as one who had attained Buddhahood, but who had voluntarily stayed back until all men could join in Enlightenment. In practice, *bodhisattvas* were agents who mediated grace, wisdom, and hope to other beings. In a theological sense their compassion (*karūna*) preserved the warm, earthy realism of early Buddhism, even as their visionary hope manifested the transcendent reality as defined by later Buddhist philosophy.

In Buddhism the Transcendent was always seen as the end of a religious quest, and therefore the images in which it was conveyed tended to be either psychological or mythological rather than metaphysical. Under Greek influence the West has become accustomed to metaphysical images, but it should not be thought that the psychological or mythological images provide any less transcendent a view of Reality.

The Indians who followed the Upaniṣadic view of the Transcendent as *Brahman* were less skeptical of metaphysical constructions than were the Buddhists. For many of the orthodox followers of the *Veda, śruti* itself, or the sound of the *Veda,* provided a revelation of *Brahman. Vāc* (speech) was a mysterious metaphysical reality which participated in the life of *Brahman* and yet appeared as a presence in the experience of man. In the *Mīmāmsā* school, this view was carried to its logical conclusion as the *śabda* (word-syllable) became the only true manifestation of the Transcendent (*Brahman*).

The later Vedāntins, such as Śaṇkara, applied Nāgārjuna's critique to the realistic metaphysics of the *Mīm-*

āṃsā and argued that the Transcendent (*Brahman*) could be known only through the Higher Truth arrived at by a vision (*jñāna*). In contrast to the Buddhists, the Vedāntins spoke of the Transcendent in positive language as the Real, the Absolute; but they agreed with Nāgārjuna that the Higher Reality was the sole reality. The Absolute (*Brahman*) was without attributes (*nirguṇa),* but for the sake of religious practice it was necessary to allow for an image of *Brahman* with attributes (*saguṇa*). *Brahman* with attributes took the form of *Īśvara,* or the one who presented himself to men as the Lord. With the doctrine of *Īśvara,* a connection was made between the highest form of transcendence and a richly varied world of mythology. Through *Īśvara* all mythological notions could become images of the Transcendent Reality.

In practice the mainstream of the Indian Tradition developed two approaches to the expression of the relationship between the mythic gods and the highest Brahman. In the sects that were collected under the name of Vaiṣṇavism, the distinction between *Brahman* and *Īśvara* is accepted and Viṣṇu is manifested, both in his form as the creative Lord of the universe, and in a variety of other forms in which he descends (*avatāra*) into the life of man to destroy evil and work for salvation. Transcendence then, for a devotee of the *avatāra* Kṛṣṇa, for instance, is a progressive realization that his friend or lover is the Lord of the universe, and even more, the Highest Reality (*Brahman*). In the sects that are associated with Śiva and Śakti, the manifestation of the Transcendent is less through a hierarchy of persons and more through a flow of power. In Kashmir Śaivism, for instance, reality is seen as a continuous flowing forth from the Highest Reality, *Śiva,* through Śiva's inseparable conscious energy, *Śakti,* to the supreme manifestation as *Sadāśiva,* then to *Īśvara,* then *Vidya* (knowledge), *Māyā* (formative principle), etc., down to the gross elements. In the *śakta* cults this energy is identified with the female principle and is manifest in various female deities. In these cults transcendence is the experience of having one's individuality consumed and one's "self" absorbed into the flow of cosmic energy which finally withdraws into the transcendent Śiva.

The Transcendent in Indian thought is a balance between the oneness of *Brahman* and the variety of mythic representations that provide the basis for cultic practice. When the two are seen together, they avoid the dangers of both an impersonal monism and an inconsistent polytheism. Taken in combination, they satisfy both the necessity of an Ultimate to which all of reality points, and the necessity of providing varied images through which man can approach the Ultimate.

The Implications

In the Indian view of life, the Transcendent determines the character of the picture. Western skepticism asks whether God exists. Indian skepticism asks whether the world exists. The West generally assumed that the world in which man lived could be seen as a cosmos with an order of its own. It was divided over the question of whether or not this order implied a creator, and over which evidence of order (cosmic, moral, historical, etc.) was most closely associated with divinity. Indian thought started with the idea that the world around did not naturally fall into an order, and that the real world lay beyond. Epistemologically the only certain reality was the subject's own consciousness, and his only hope was to free his consciousness from the experiences of multiplicity.

The Transcendent presents itself in man's experience as an umbrella of meaning. Life consists, not in the sum total of the bits and pieces that lie in front of us, but in the contours of the shadow that the Transcendent throws over us. Man's life does not naturally fit into the shaded contours of the umbrella's shadow, and as a result, experience of the bits and pieces is painful (*duḥkha*). But in the final analysis the shadow envelops all of life. Life in the shadow of the Transcendent is defined, not in terms of the activity of man or the activity of the gods, but in terms of the cessation of activity and the recognition of the shadow. The Transcendent does not actively create the world, but rather allows the world to evolve as a screen of activity veiling the truth of the Absolute. As man comes to understand himself and the world around him the veil fades from view and only the Transcendent One remains.

A second implication of the Indian understanding of the Transcendent is that it is the Transcendent that gives meaning to the individual's life. While the Transcendent pervades all of life, it also reveals itself to individuals in very specific forms. In some theological systems "transcendence" is taken to mean an absence of the divine that leaves man with a feeling of fear and alienation. This interpretation is based on the assumption of a divine-human polarity. The Indian conception of "transcendence" goes behind this polarity and sees the Transcendent as encompassing man within itself. In this sense the Transcendent is also immanent and appears as a presence in the life of men. The imagery, however, is not so much that of the divine taking on the likeness of men, but that of the continual presence of something like the Garden of Paradise in which the gods are free to sport (*līlā*) with men.

The need to see the Transcendent as a presence within the life of man has led to a great variety of divine manifestations in India. If the Transcendent is to become a presence in all of life, then the forms of his expression will have to be as varied as life itself. It will have to be a boar (Varāha) rescuing the Earth from the cosmic waters. It will have to be a lover (Kṛṣṇa) entering the heart of the beloved. It will have to be the cosmic dance (Śiva Naṭaraja) of creation, preservation, destruction, rest, and recreation. And it will have to be whatever else will give birth to an individual's awareness of that which lies beyond the bits and pieces before him. The Transcendent transforms all parts of life into symbols of itself so that every man finds himself in the presence of that which transcends.

The meaning of man's life consists in his awareness of the presence of the Transcendent. For the Buddhist this involved following the "path"; for the devotee of Kṛṣṇa, passion for his Lord; for the Śaivite, absorption in the cosmic dance. For each man the meaning would differ, depending on the form in which the Transcendent had been made manifest to him. Man was not left alone to make his own meaning or establish his own "values," but neither was he forced into a single mold of goodness determined by a specific form of revelation. The shadow of the Transcendent provided all of life with meaning, but men responding to the different manifestations of the

Transcendent perceived that meaning in a variety of ways.

Finally, the idea of the Transcendent provided man with a dimension of hope. As experienced by man, the Transcendent is an experience of potentiality. The experience of *duḥkha* within the world of *samsāra* will eventually be transformed into the experience of *ānanda* (bliss) within the world of *Brahman*.

In its ontological status, *Brahman* is conceived of as static being. It is beyond the realm of change, and the categories of space and time do not apply to it. But the religious life of the individual is not a simple deduction from the ontological situation. Man is in reality a part of *Brahman*, but in his present structure of experience, his oneness with *Brahman* is veiled from him by the world of *samsāra*. Thus, in an experiential sense, oneness with *Brahman* is a potential reality which becomes the object of man's quest.

The hope that is born of the potential oneness with *Brahman* has nothing to do with success in history. It does not see an order of events in history as a manifestation of divine perfection, but neither does it see history as an expression of evil and disorder requiring an apocalyptic intervention. History represents the sport of the gods, but the real basis of hope lies not in that sport but in man's potential oneness with that which transcends. Man within history catches glimpses of the Transcendent, and with those glimpses, all of life is oriented around a new quest. With the quest begun, much of life appears as an experience of *duḥkha* (pain), for man carries within his heart the burden of the hope of transcendence. While the hope represents a burden, it also represents an evidence of new life which will be fulfilled when the veil of change is finally left aside.

When the awareness of the Transcendent dawns, the Indian's whole view of life is transformed. The reality of the Transcendent becomes a shadow that shows up the passing ephemeral nature of the world of change. But the reality of the Transcendent not only casts a shadow over the life of man; it also provides him with meaning and hope. Meaning is conveyed to man not only in terms of the shadow which affects all but also in terms of the many individual patterns which the different manifestations of the Transcendent have set forth. Finally, the Transcendent gives men hope, because all of life is reoriented around the individual's potential oneness with *Brahman*. These patterns of meaning and this sense of hope do not give a rigidity or otherworldliness to the Indian understanding of life, but they do give it an order and purposiveness which finally triumphs over the sense of painful disorder in which life was first conceived.

8

Mokṣa: Salvation

The Phenomena

The final stage in the experience of "transcendence" is salvation or release itself. It is difficult to describe the concept of salvation because it must be described in the language of the future. Salvation is a state which is anticipated rather than an experience which has already been realized. Religious traditions speak of salvation in three ways. They define it as a goal; they outline the "way" which leads to that goal; and they provide a place for men who have already attained the state of salvation. My outline of the phenomena of the Indian Tradition will follow this threefold pattern.

The radical disjunction between the everyday life of man and the state of salvation was set forth most clearly by the Buddha when he outlined his four noble truths. The analysis of life in the first two truths ("All of life is painfulness"; and "Painfulness arises from change or flux") does not provide any ground for hope or salvation. The third truth unexpectedly affirms that there can be a total cessation of pain (*duḥkha*). Suddenly the whole perspective of man's life is changed, for *Nirvāna,* or the total cessation of pain, becomes a positive state of salvation toward which all of life should be directed. By defining salvation in terms of the silence of the "other shore," the concept of *Nirvāna* requires that salvation be conceived of as a total "transcendence" of the world of change and not as a correction or improvement thereof. Salvation in this definition takes man beyond the world of subjects and objects altogether and into a condition which totally transcends this world.

In a manner which closely parallels that of the Buddhists, the Upaniṣads speak of salvation in terms of *mokṣa* (release). This concept, too, begins with an analysis of *samsāra* and sees the insights that lead to an awareness of the Transcendent (*Brahman*) as in themselves capable of giving man release (*mokṣa*) from *samsāra.* The emphasis in the term *mokṣa* is negative, in that it refers to the breaking of the ties of repeated existence in *samsāra,* but, like the Buddhist term *Nirvāna,* it sees salvation as a complete transcendence of the world of *samsāra.*

The concept of *mokṣa* became a framework within which a number of differing emphases in the conception of salvation were developed. The Vedānta theologians saw salvation as the self's (*ātman's*) realization of its oneness with *Brahman* and they described this realization as an experience of *sat* (being)—*cit* (consciousness)—*ānanda* (bliss). This interpretation sees salvation primarily as a state of true Being, free from the illusory reality of *māyā.* A second interpretation is set forth by the Sāṃkhya and Yoga schools, which see salvation as the *kevala* (aloneness), which comes to the *puruṣa* (conscious self) when it is separated from the evolving *prakṛti.* This interpretation emphasizes the fact that salvation is the freeing of the "self" or "subject" from the "other" reality of "objects" and constant transformation. Man is not saved in the sense that he is transferred into a perfect expression of the world of objects, but in that he realizes in his self-consciousness his true nature as a conscious subject. A third interpretation of *mokṣa* envisaged salvation as union with the Lord of devotion. In this interpretation the emphasis is on the blissful identity with the Lord, but again the final state envisaged is one which totally transcends the scene of *samsāra* as both the individual and the world are reabsorbed in the play (*līlā*) of the Lord.

Because of the practical nature of Indian religion, the "way" to salvation often received more attention than the idea of salvation itself. The Buddha, after affirming the possibility of *Nirvāna* in the third truth, went on in the fourth truth to outline an eightfold path to salvation. This path consisted of a series of psychological stages that are not exactly parallel to any other "way" set forth in India but contain elements of both Yoga discipline and the philosophical quest for mystical insight. The steps begin with an orientation according to "right views" and "right intentions," then move through "right livelihood," "right words" and "right actions," and finally conclude with the three mystical stages of "right effort," "right mindfulness," and "right meditation." In practice, the specificity of this path seemed to dominate the minds of the Theravāda ("Southern") monks and obscure the transcendent goal of *Nirvāna.* The schools of Mahāyāna ("Northern") Buddhism quietly ignored this path and substituted philosophical and devotional alternatives.

The schools of Vedānta attempted to follow as closely as possible the teachings of the Upaniṣads and to resist the development of separate cultic "ways" to salvation on the ground that no "way" could adequately anticipate the Transcendent Absolute, *Brahman.* Nevertheless, others speak of the way of Vedānta as a "way" of *jñāna* (knowledge) because it is through insights into the limitations of experienced reality that a man is led beyond to an awareness of his identity with *Brahman.*

One of the problems with the "way" of knowledge as outlined in the Vedānta is that it does not provide very concrete direction for man's stay in the world of *samsāra.* In the *Bhagavad Gītā,* Arjuna raises this question when he says he does not know how to act as he faces the battlefield. Kṛṣṇa, as his charioteer and teacher, sets forth an interpretation by which his action (*karma*) in battle becomes a "way" to salvation. Arjuna should understand that the only Reality is *Brahman,* and that neither slaying nor nonslaying affects the self (*ātman*) of a man. Secondly, he should realize that social and political relationships should be determined, not by any self-involvement that he might mistakenly feel, but by the objective law of *dharma.* Finally, if he realizes both of these truths, he will have discovered the true nature of the "self" (*ātman*) as consciousness free from its objects. Having discovered this, he will be able to act with detachment, and his action will be a "way" of salvation to him because it will be an affirmation of the sole reality of *Brahman.* The man who acts with detachment is said to follow the "way" of the *karma yogin.*

Both the "way" of *jñāna* and the "way" of the *karma yogin* emphasize the goal of salvation and hesitate to provide too detailed or specific a "way." Other schools of *yoga* developed an elaborate "way" rooted in the discipline of the bodily, respiratory, and mental activities. The *Yoga Sūtras* of Pātanjali carefully relate this discipline to the goal of separateness (*kevala*) so that the *yogin* moves beyond the discipline into the dimension of the Transcendent. In practice, however, many later schools of *yoga* have emphasized the discipline and have sometimes even allowed asceticism to become an end in itself.

The most popular "way" to salvation in India was through devotion (*bhakti*) to a Lord. Sectarian groups that practiced devotion seem to have grown up in a variety of forms all over India. These groups were gradually brought into the mainstream of Indian religion, where they accepted the framework of *samsāra* and the idea of salvation as *mokṣa,* but they continued to see devotion as the best means to the attainment of that goal. Śaṇkara, the great eighth-century theologian, provided for the different views of the goal and the "way" by distinguishing two levels of truth. This arrangement allowed Śaṇkara to be a rigid non-dualist (*advaitin*) philosophically while remaining a devout Śaivite religiously. Some Śaivites could not accept Śaṇkara's "two truth" solution and insisted that the purest *advaita* (non-duality) was the one which saw Śiva as the sole reality. They saw Śiva manifest in a series of emanations, all of which would again be withdrawn into himself with not even the illusion (*māyā*) remaining outside him. The devotee worshiped the power (*śakta)* manifest in the symbol of the *liṇga* (phallus); or he worshiped the *Śiva Natarāja* (Dancing Śiva), who moved the cosmic cycle in its five stages; or he meditated with Śiva's consort Pārvatī on the ascetic form of the god. But finally, the devotee (*paśu*) found himself absorbed in Śiva, his Lord (*Pati*), and his bonds (*pāśa*) were released as he became one with the transcendent Lord.

The devotion of the Vaiṣṇavite schools was generally

warmer and more personal than that of the Śaivite schools. Rāmānuja, a theologian of the eleventh century, was a devout Vaiṣṇavite who attempted to bring his devotion into line with the goal of non-duality (*advaita*). He worked out a compromise which was called *Viśiṣṭādvaita* or "oneness with difference," for he argued that both the souls and the world are partially real, in the sense that they provide the "body" for the "soul" which is *Brahman*. In this arrangement, *Brahman* could manifest himself as the Lord (*Īśvara*), and devotion (*bhakti*) to him could be seen as a "way" to *mokṣa* (release). In this interpretation salvation is thought of primarily as the bliss (*ānanda*) of union with the Lord. Around this idea of devotion Vaiṣṇavism has developed a variety of differing "ways" to salvation. Some see man as dust and ashes, awaiting the grace of the Lord (as a newborn kitten awaits its mother's mouth); others see man clinging to the Lord (as a baby monkey clings to its mother). The Lord is seen by some as the creator of the cosmos; by others as the divine lover for whom Rādha and the cowherd girls long; and by others as Rāma the sovereign ruler and judge. In many of these sects the emphasis is on the "way" of devotion, so that the final goal of *mokṣa* is obscured; but in each the theological statements point beyond the "way" to the final release from *samsāra* and the absorption into *Brahman*.

A third and final evidence of the Indian's idea of salvation can be seen in the role given to those who have already attained release. Generally speaking, Indian theology maintains that salvation is totally beyond and cannot be manifest as a particular style of life within this world. In practice, however, there was a clear hierarchy of spiritual attainment which distinguished men, and a man normally chose someone whom he considered enlightened to guide him on his way to salvation. The person so chosen was called a *guru,* and his follower, a *chela.* The *guru* within the orthodox tradition would deny that he had attained release and thus would preserve the transcendent character of the goal, but the *chela's* devotion to his "holy man" affirmed the position that at least in some measure the Transcendent could be embodied in the life of men.

The personification of salvation varied according to the interpretation of the "way" which it was intended to represent. The Jain image of salvation is personified in the *Tīrthankara* (Ford Crosser), who has removed all the *karmas* of this world and, freed of this burden, has floated weightlessly to a fixed abode in the heavens. The Buddhist *arhat* (Noble One) attains his own release but also serves as an example and teachers for others. The Buddha (The Enlightened One) spent much of his life as an active teacher, but the *arhat* was thought of as only partially fulfilling the ideal of the Buddha. Mahāyāna Buddhism sought to restore the active role of the ideal by introducing the idea of the *bodhisattva,* the Enlightened One, who out of compassion (*karūna*) for all creatures waited on the threshold of *Nirvāna* until salvation was attained by all. As portrayed in art, the images of the *Buddha* and the *bodhisattvas* provided a very vivid picture of the state of the Enlightened.

The Vedānta theologians saw salvation as total absorption in *Brahman* and were therefore reluctant to allow for a personification of that state. They did allow for the possibility of a *jīvanmukta,* or a man who continued to live after his release from *samsāra.* Most of the texts give very little importance to this state, and one gets the impression that it might be possible only in the final, or *Sannyāsin,* stage of life. However, the *Gītā* pictures a *karma yogin* as a man active in this world, and the twentieth-century philosopher Aurobindo works out an idea of the *jīvanmukta* who descends from the highest knowledge of *Brahman* to activity within every order of life. In practice most men thought of salvation as it was personified in their teacher or the Lord of their devotion. The Śaivite sought salvation as personified in the cosmic power and free activity of Dancing Śiva; the devotee of Kṛṣṇa sought to realize the warm humanity and joyful sport of the Lord; and the follower of *Yoga* sought to realize the cool detachment of the master *Yogin.* These personifications of salvation were aids along the "way," but finally every man had to pass beyond both the personification and the "way" and know salvation as a total release (*mokṣa*) from the world of *samsāra* and an entrance into the Transcendent where all forms are left behind.

The Implications

What general statements can be made about the contribution that the Indian idea of salvation (*mokṣa*) makes to the understanding of human experience? The most obvious effect which the idea of *mokṣa* has on experience is that it turns all of life into an expectation. Nothing is just what it appears to be, and life's possibilities are not as closed as they seem. Something else is the end of life, and all of experience, if rightly understood, points beyond itself.

The hope that characterizes Indian thought has been difficult for Westerners to understand. Christian hope arises from the Easter triumph over the power of evil which had come to reign over the world because of the fall of man. As a variation on this theme, the Marxist and "liberal" notions of progress have described life as a historical struggle in which man learns the techniques by which to gain his freedom and lead the right in triumph. Seen in this perspective, hope is almost identical with triumph and is seen in opposition to the evil which pervades life.

The Indian idea of hope is built on an expectation of salvation that pervades all of life. Life has never been marred by radical evil, and so the quest for salvation is not a struggle leading to a triumph, but a patient determination to remove the chaff which hides the kernel of truth. With the fear of evil removed, there is not the nagging self-doubt which cripples hope; and with the concern with triumph absent, there is no need to crush the opposition in order to realize the future. Nature is basically good, and man's hope consists not in triumphing over it, but in reveling in its rhythms and discovering the ray of light which lies behind it. Man's future is a genuinely open one, because the deepest reality is about to be revealed. This expectation releases man from the bondage of this world, but also transforms this world into a scene of preparation for that which is to come.

The second major contribution of the doctrine of salvation to the understanding of experience is that it makes all of life a preparation for *mokṣa*. Life, viewed as a preparation for *mokṣa,* could be seen in a number of ways. It could be seen as a domain of evil that must be escaped as soon as possible. This view has been known in many cultures, but was not characteristic of India except in the heterodox Jain sect, which believed that all activity was evil and man was released only when present activity ceased and the effect of all past activity was expelled. A second possibility would be to see this life as a testing ground where men choose between good and evil. This view has led to the development of puritanical movements in many religious traditions, but puritanism had very little place in the Indian tradition. Both of these views can be described as "otherworldly," for the first one actively rejects this life; and the second, while calling for action in this world, defines that action in accord with a set of values that are meaningful in terms of another world. Another view of this life as a preparation for salvation (*mokṣa*) would be one which accepted the structures of this world but ordered them all to the pursuit of a single goal. This would be the Indian view.

When the Indian interprets life so as to see it as a preparation for *mokṣa* (salvation), he is affirming that life has meaning. Man is not in the grip of evil or even in a neutral battleground between good and evil. Man is somewhere in the garden of god, but he has yet to make his way to the source of life. The meaning of his life is to be found in the charting out of the path through the garden and the gradual rise from the obvious levels of experience to those which will free him from the world of change. The stages on this garden path are not unlike the hierarchy in the spiritual life as understood by Western mysticism. In both cases the structures of this life are seen as meaningful because they develop a pattern of growth which leads on to salvation. The Indians went much farther than their Western counterparts, for while the latter suggested a hierarchy of society within the monastery or the clergy or within an ideal society such as that suggested by Plato, the Indians actually developed their whole social theory as a structure preparatory to salvation. Both the four castes and the four stages in the life of the individual were intended to provide a preparatory framework on which a man could move along toward salvation. Life as a preparation for *mokṣa* was not seen as an unimportant waiting station, or as a testing ground, but as part of a total scheme of meaning. In the total scheme, every detail of life took on an importance and a relevance that could not be lost. Man hadn't the responsibility and the seriousness that goes with the puritan picture of life as a battleground of good and evil. But neither did he see his life as a flurry of activity signifying nothing. Life was play within the garden, but it was play that moved toward a goal.

The third and final implication for experience that arises from the Indian understanding of salvation is that experience can become a manifestation of divinity. Other traditions make similar claims. In Zen it is possible to experience *satori,* and in Christianity there are "saints," and in holiness sects there are those who have been "sanctified." In most cases these are seen as isolated and primarily subjective experiences.

The holy men of India are not thought of as exceptional, but as the norm toward which all men move. Life is not a drab scene or a closed system from which only a few escape to experience bliss. All men are potentially holy men; therefore the experience of all is pervaded with that sense of potential divinity.

From the perspective of the end, all of experience blends into one. The "acceptance" of the structures of *samsāra* is but another side of the quest for "transcendence." The acceptance of the womb, the maintenance of *dharma,* and the refinement of culture are but stages in the discovery of the "self." The obedience to tradition, and the quest for the self, for the Transcendent, and for the final experience of *mokṣa* are simply deeper levels of "self"-awareness. In the end, they all become part of a theology of joy as we realize that we are that which we sought. Experience finally dissolves, and the experiencer, the "self," stands free of all duality. His joy lies, not alone in his escape, but in the depth of awareness given by experience. All of life was serious, because it pointed to an end; but all of life was also joy, because it was really a scene for the manifestation of the divine.

Conclusions on Part Two

The Indian quest for "transcendence" stands out as one of the most distinctive expressions of the religious experience of mankind. It places an emphasis on the "developing self-awareness" which marks it off from the religious experience found in other traditions. While this emphasis doubtless causes the Indian Tradition to give less attention to some other aspects of experience, it does allow it to solve certain central problems in the nature of human experiencing.

The first problem that the Indian emphasis on experience as "developing self-awareness" tackles is the problem of relating the religious quest for "that which might be" with an acceptance of "life as it is." How is it possible to maintain a transcendental goal for human experience without ignoring this world?

Many traditions have not focused attention on this problem, and the result is that, in those traditions, ends and means tend to shift back and forth and become confused one with another. Sometimes the Beyond becomes an all-encompassing goal, which leads to a disparagement of "life as it is." Sometimes a reaction sets in against this overemphasis on the Transcendent, and a "secular" theology develops that tries to see "life as it might be" in terms of the struggle within "life as it is." Sometimes a doctrine such as the "divine providence" is used as a stimulus of, and justification for, the wealth and power of a specific social community. At other times a serious economic or political imbalance gives rise to a call for economic or political change, such as that embodied in the Marxist call for a "classless society," or the North American quest for "freedom;" and these economic and political quests are gradually expressed in religious terms, as if they were the highest goals of human existence. The dangers inherent in this constant shifting back and forth between "life as it is" and "life as it might be" are numerous. In some situations, religion is used as a means for attaining worldly goals. In other situations, economic or political programs take on an aura of divine sanction and cease to be subject to normal criticism. In general there is neither a concentration on practical solutions to problems in this world nor a concentration on the nature of the spiritual quest.

The Indian solution to these problems is its emphasis on "tradition." "Tradition" establishes a pattern of relationship between "life as it is" and "life as it might be," but insists that the two be kept distinct. The first without the second is shallow and inevitably leads to some form of oppression. The second without the first would be a false escapism. If the first seeks to include the second within itself, it is only using the divine to extend the range of its oppressive power. If the second seeks to include the first within itself, it destroys the social and psychological rootage from which life springs forth, and makes the spiritual quest a rootless sprout which dies quickly.

The first important contribution of "tradition" is a rootedness for the spiritual quest. Man seeking the Transcendent is not cut off from his mother's womb, his social context, or the philosophy, occupation, and art which make up his adult culture. All of these are a necessary part of his spiritual quest and are a part of the sages' reinterpretation of human experience received by the individual as "tradition." While this "tradition" is defined in such a flexible way that almost any man's experience can be reinterpreted so as to help him on the way, it would not be possible to think of the spiritual quest apart from such rootage. Man enters upon the higher quest only insofar as his heritage provides him rootage. In this sense the concept of "tradition" encourages the most careful possible development of the psychological, social, and cultural bases of life. As the raw material of "tradition," they serve as an essential element in the spiritual quest itself, an element without which the quest would quickly fade.

The second important contribution of "tradition" is that it gives the individual an "orientation" toward the Transcendent. "Tradition" is, broadly speaking, a "revelation," a manifestation of the Transcendent within the categories of this world. "Tradition" is not simply a record of human experience, but it is the enlightened sages' vision of the meaning of life as an orientation toward that which Transcends. To put it in still another phrase, "tradition" is an intimation of the Transcendent which is received in the forms of this life. In this sense "tradition" is a continuing part of the "developing self-awareness" of the individual and not a preliminary to it. It is the root of the plant, and its strength and character are part of the strength and character of the whole spiritual growth.

The Western tension between religious authority and social and political relevance seems to the Indian to be born of confusion. To make social and political relevance the end of human existence and an adequate guide for all religious life is to deny entirely the higher quest and therefore also much of human experience. On the other hand, for religious authorities to dictate social or political behavior patterns is to outstep their role as definers of the "orientation" toward the Transcendent. In the "traditionalist" framework, social and political relevance and sagely authority are interdependent aspects of one structure. While the first produces the actual rootage from which the spiritual quest gains strength, the second defines the goal toward which that quest is directed. When the first is taken as a goal or the second as a source of strength, neither relevance nor direction results. But when they work together as interdependent parts of the structure of "tradition," the quest for the Transcendent has both vitality and direction. As seen in the light of "tradition," true humanity includes simultaneously both social obligation and a higher quest. When both are seen in this kind of interdependence, no part of man's experience is set aside as irrelevant, but all carry him on to his highest goal.

The second problem in human experience that is tackled in a theology of "developing self-awareness" is the problem of the locale of religious life. How is it possible for the Transcendent to grow and develop within the life of man?

The Indian emphasis on the "self" as the locale for the manifestation of the Transcendent has sometimes led to the mistaken notion that the Indian relies on his own resources for salvation. This mistake is a result of the very different meanings given to the term "self" in Western religious thought and in Indian religious thought. To speak about the "self" in the Western context is to speak about a center of willed autonomy. In the strictest sense that center is considered an expression of "sin" and a rebellion against the Will which created the world. As a result, the life of the religious subject is spoken of somewhat hesitantly, even though the Psalmist spoke at length about the state of his "soul" and the apostle Paul enjoyed speaking about the development of his "spirit."

In the Indian view, the "self" is a manifestation of consciousness. As such, it is not set over against other forms of consciousness, but shares with them in a common awareness. One shares consciousness with one's fellow creatures on the one hand, and with the Transcendent on the other. Thus in one's "developing self-awareness," one is not moving away from one's fellows, nor is one taking over divine prerogatives. One is simply moving into a greater fullness in which all share.

The quest for the Transcendent is often described in Indian imagery as similar to the growth of a tree. Deep rootage is important, as is the life and direction provided by the sun for the branches above. But in the final analysis, a tree is only as strong as its trunk. It is in the developing strength of the trunk that the depth of rootage and the life of the sun are manifest.

To hold that it is in the life of the "self" that "transcendence" becomes manifest does not mean that the

Indian is limited to his own resources along the spiritual way. Actually he is being transformed out of his earlier individuality, first of all by his discovery that the "self" (*ātman*) is not limited to the forms of his own space and time, and eventually by the awareness that he is being reabsorbed into the all-pervading consciousness (*Brahman*). This transformation is in every way a product of the resources of the Transcendent in whose light all is changed.

Where the Indian Tradition is distinctive is in its emphasis on the higher quest as "development" and "growth." Salvation for the Indian could never consist of flashes from another world inadvertently received in this world. There are many different gods with many different approaches to their devotees; but the crucial thing is not so much the nature of their activity, but the nature of the resultant spiritual growth which they leave behind. It is in the developing "self" that the Transcendent grows and manifests itself.

By interpreting the quest for "transcendence" in terms of the developing life of the "self," the Indian Tradition has not had to sacrifice either the personality of the individual or the ultimacy of the Transcendent. The individual is not thought of as dust and ashes which disappear so quickly before the divine light that all higher experience is immediately lost. Neither is a romantic affirmation of individuality allowed to obscure the all-encompassing character of the Ultimate. By seeing the "self" as both an individual consciousness and a being which is potentially one with the highest Reality, the theology of "developing self-awareness" at the same time strengthens the concept of personality and provides a channel for understanding that which is Ultimate.

Finally, the theology of a "developing self-awareness" emphasizes the change in the nature of man by the end of the spiritual quest. How is it possible for man to really enter into a life that "transcends" this world?

In a way, all religious systems promise a transformed existence. Sometimes the goal is expressed negatively as a release from sin or from bondage of some sort. Sometimes it is expressed in terms of a promise of a separate land, a new type of kingdom, an endowment with power, or a state of blissful enjoyment. The difference between these expressions of religious hope and the Indian goal is that the latter emphasizes the idea that the end of the quest is not a corrected model of this world, but a new, "transcendent," state.

Actually this Indian hope probably appears more "unusual" to modern Western men than it should. There is plenty on transcendental hope in the Biblical literature, but the mythology of heaven and hell in which it was expressed in the Western Religious Tradition gradually fell into disrepute, and with it went some of the earlier hopefulness about the future. The result was that the struggles of the present were projected into the future, and the most that could be expected was a slight improvement. Now that biological and psychological research has begun to demonstrate the great potentialities of both body and mind, the closed universe of recent Western religious thought is beginning to open up again. It would seem inevitable that in some form or other, transcendental hope would be part of that new openness.

In the Indian Tradition there is a strong emphasis on the "otherness" of the final hope. The Buddha spoke of *Nirvāna* as an "other" shore, to be known only after the crossing of the mysterious stream. The purpose of this emphasis was to maintain the ultimacy of the Transcendent and the mysterious openness of the individual's quest.

But in contrast to the "otherness" of the goal is the Indian recognition of the fruits of the divine life. The *bodhisattvas* were active expressions of the meaning of Enlightenment as they sought to help others along the way. But while few of the "holy men" are active in that sense, all serve as living personifications of the goal and as evidence of the unlimited potentiality of the liberated consciousness.

The Indian description of the highest experience sought to avoid the dangers, on the one hand, of making it sound like an empty fruitless ending, and on the other, of making it a scene of pleasure that had no ultimacy. What they finally succeed in doing is to present a goal, the ultimacy of which could hardly be questioned, and the quest for which directs the higher life of man. If the nature of that life is not described in terms of the longings of this world, it is because it is seen in terms of an utter transformation and absorption in the Transcendent. The end of man is higher than even his vision can take him, but his quest is rooted in the carefully developed experience of the "self" and the solid foundation of "tradition." Only the utter "transcendence" of the end will be true to the intimations of the Transcendent which enriched so much of his earlier experience.

A theology of "developing self-awareness" involves the interpretation of a wide range of experiences. It organizes each experience into a central focus which grows upward to the final absorption in the Transcendent but never minimizes the stages along the way. By using "tradition" to forge a relationship between life "as it is" and the quest for life "as it might be," it assures that none of the ordinary life of man is brushed aside. By insisting that the quest be ordered in terms of the developing life of the "self," the Tradition provides that quest with a structure and content which makes easy, false, and otherworldly interpretations of the "way" impossible. Finally, by insisting that the potentiality of the quest remain unmeasured, the Tradition guarantees that the Transcendent will not be compromised, and that a mysterious wonder and direction will remain in the religious life of man.

In the total Indian religious experience, the theology of "experience" balances the theology of "developing self-awareness." The one gives the religious life a warm human relevance, and the other gives it a direction and purpose. The first alone would be cheap and the second alone, hollow. Together they provide the individual with a fullness of life which is both rich in content and strong in development.

This is the religious experience of man as the Indian Tradition has formulated it. What lessons it bears for men outside that Tradition remains to be seen.

EPILOGUE

Indian Religion in the West

Is the new Western appropriation of Indian religion legitimate? This question is on many minds but is essentially unanswerable, both because of the great diversity among those attracted to Indian religion and because it is hard to know who has a right to say what is legitimate in this area. The mass media have associated the whole of the hippie movement with India. Orthodox Indians hearing that they are associated with drugs, sexual freedom, and unwashed bodies vigorously protest. But the hippie of the mass media and the Indian who would feel a need to defend his Tradition are hardly representative of either side in the encounter. The Westerner attracted by Indian religion might be a hippie, a serious undergraduate, a thoughtful citizen repelled by violence, a liberal housewife, an imaginative theologian, or a creative artist. He might read quietly, take a vigorous role in the reexamination of his culture, or be a member of one of the cultic communities of guruism, yogism, etc. On the other hand, the India that these people love may be the India of an earlier day, an India of warm erotic art and music, an India of rigidly prescribed thought or ritual, or an India that provides a cultic path to salvation. No Indian spokesman can legitimately represent all of these aspects of India, any more than any one characteristic can accurately describe the variety of Westerners who now look to India for guidance.

Are there any general statements that can be made about this new and interesting religious development—the Western attraction to Indian religion? One thing that is reasonably obvious, but needs to be seen more clearly, is that this is a Western religious phenomenon and not an Indian one. When the Ramakrishna Mission organized missions to the West in the early part of this century, the missions were a part of the Indian Tradition even though in a new form. While these missions have survived, they have had very little to do with the contemporary Western interest in India. This interest arose because of cultural and theological problems in the West, and it is legitimate or illegitimate to the extent that it results in solutions to those problems.

What are the Western religious problems that have given rise to an interest in Indian religion? This question raises very profound issues in the Western Religious Tradition, which are not the proper subject of the present study. Here we will simply attempt to indicate the immediate and obvious forms in which this interest has arisen, and why it is that the Indian tradition has seemed a likely place to seek help.

While a general loosening of the ties of the Western Tradition make men open to a variety of other traditions, certain other, more particular sociological and psychological factors turn certain men and women in the direction of one of the available religious traditions. Thus it was the need for an aggressive equalitarian religion that led some black Americans to Islam. On the other hand, it was the need for an escapist quietude which led affluent intelligent individualists to Zen. In a similar way, it is the need for a radical alternative to the violent and impersonal technology produced by the myth of progress which has turned large numbers of the young toward India. Many of those who are disaffected by the violent impersonality of their society remain negative and are tempted into violence themselves, while many others turn to romantic avenues of personal escape and integrity. But the thoughtful recognize that solid alternatives must be suggested, and the most thoughtful recognize that alternate models that human societies have created elsewhere may be a useful place to begin.

India comes into this quest somewhere between the romantic escape and the dawning awareness that some positive structure must be read into the picture one has of human experience. The warm, pulsating music of India is somehow strengthening after the themes of conflict and tragedy in one's own music. When the attention is turned to the other art forms of painting, sculpture, or the dance, this awareness is confirmed by the presence of the divine within the structures of life. Kṛṣṇa plays with the girls in the garden from which Adam and Eve were driven out; the Buddha or Bodhisattva sits in a serenity of silence and compassion; or the dancer acts out the *līlā* (sport) of God in fashioning this world. The awareness conveyed by this art raises important theological questions, but it is not initially understood at that level. Initially it is a confirmation of human experience itself; of the awareness that life is beautiful; and that man can be more than a cog in a violent and impersonal system.

The awareness of human experience that Westerners

see manifest in the Indian Tradition raises two other very serious questions. The first of these questions has to do with the understanding of the relation between nature, society, and man. Until fairly recently it was universally assumed that, through research into the natural world, man had made great progress in mastering that world and that, through similar research into society, man would learn all the mechanisms in human behavior. This confidence was supported by Christian theological theories that adjusted to a variety of needs and saw God as nature's law; as change itself; and finally as the sanctifier of historical power. It has suddenly dawned on people that this theory of the relation between nature, society, and man must be somehow awry. Scientific skill seems to lead to pollution and violence and social scientific skill seems unable to reorganize cities or establish political or economic relations between nations that can sustain order.

India's ability to speak to the question of the location of order between nature, society, and man has not yet emerged as a major manifestation of her impact. It is easier to see how the warmth of Indian music can convey the sense of a framework for human experience than it is to see how the hierarchical Indian caste system can help those crying for a "democratic society" to realize their end. Nevertheless, the concept of *dharma* does establish an alternative view of the relation between the psychological, social, and natural orders that is beginning to attract some attention. An order that is defined in terms of the range of possible and desirable psychological or human arrangements is bound to create a very different society from one that is defined in terms of the possible developments of the physical order. It may be possible to fly to outer space, but in an order of *dharma* that would not be sufficient reason for doing it. We have grown unaccustomed to giving top priority to questions such as what kind of environment is necessary for children and to the ordering of society and nature to provide that environment. The order of *dharma* may seem remote from the everyday problems of a technological society, but to those who are willing to hold up all until a decent set of priorities are developed, the order of *dharma* provides an interesting possible framework.

Finally, the Western interest in Indian religion is bound to reopen the question of the nature of salvation. In some ways this issue has been raised more clearly than the previous question of *dharma*. A generation of Westerners have been saying that life is limited to what we know in our moment on the stage of history and that salvation should be interpreted to mean an improvement in the stage props. The European world was so devastated by the Second World War that it began to question this position, and Vietnam and other problems have begun to make Americans, too, doubt if they are enjoying the millennium. An overconfident generation in the West thought India "pessimistic" and "life-denying," but a new generation is examining the mystery that lies behind *Yoga* technique and other supernormal experiences. The question is again open as to whether life has no exit or whether man's experience is but a small part of a vast mystery.

The Buddha made a careful examination of experience and concluded not only that there was a mystery beyond but in the light of that mystery our life was put in a shade. He stated this in a beautifully simple way when he said "all of life is painfulness" and held out the hope of

Nirvāna. The Indian Tradition took up his suggestion and developed thorough analyses of human experience, both as an "acceptance" of the order of *samsāra* and as a "transcendence" of that order in the movement to salvation. Our human existence takes place on a different stage, but the issues raised by the Buddha still seem hauntingly relevant. Could it be that the quest for salvation is to begin again?

GLOSSARY

Note on Pronunciation: In Sanskrit a letter is always pronounced in the same way. Each syllable should be pronounced as a separate unit. The long form of the vowel is always indicated. For instance "a" is always like the vowel in the word "cut," and "ā" always as in "car." There is an extra vowel "ṛ" which is pronounced like "ri." There are a number of different nasals ("m's" and "n's"), but they would normally not be distinguished by the English ear. The same is true of the two "t's" and "d's." The "g" is the English hard "g" as in "gate." There are three "s's." The plain "s" is pronounced as in "see." The "ṣ" is pronounced "sh" as in "shoot." The "ś" is pronounced somewhere between the other two.

Abhidharma	A school of "southern" Buddhism which believed that reality was made up of many separate particles called *"dharmas."*
Advaita	"Non-dual" school of philosophy. Its best-known representative was Śaṇkara.
Ājīvakas	An early religious movement that tended toward fatalism.
ānanda	Bliss.
anātman	Soullessness. A Buddhist doctrine.

Āraṇyaka	Ancient Vedic texts usually set between the Brahmāṇas and the Upaniṣads.
arhat	Religious ideal of "southern" Buddhism.
artha	Material well-being. The second of the four "ends of man."
Arthaśāstra	Text on the "science of politics." The best-known example is by Kautilya.
āśramas	The four stages in the development of the life of man: student, householder, retired man, and ascetic.
asura	Awesome, mysterious and usually malevolent "power." Especially Ṛg Vedic.
Ātman	The name for Ultimate Reality when seen as subjective consciousness or the "Self."
avatāra	"To descend." The forms the god Viṣṇu assumed when coming into the world.
avidyā	"A-vidyā." The absence of knowledge; ignorance.
Bhagavad Gītā	The most important religious text in the Indian Tradition; attached to the *Mahābhārata* epic. Teaches obedience to *dharma* and devotion to Lord Kṛṣṇa.
Bhāgavata Purāṇa	A medieval text of "mythological history," encouraging devotion to Kṛṣṇa.
bhajan	Devotional hymn.

Bhārat Mātā	A popular expression meaning "Mother India."
Bhārat Nāṭyam	The classical dance style of India.
bhāṣya	Commentary on religious texts.
bodhisattva	Mahāyāna Buddhist ideal. One who has earned Enlightenment but chooses to remain in this world until all creatures have been enlightened.
Brahman	The usual name for Ultimate Reality.
brāhman	The name of the priestly caste. The highest caste in the hierarchy.
Brahmāṇa	Ancient Vedic texts of priestly ritual.
chela	Disciple.
daṇḍa	The scepter of power wielded by the king.
darśānas	Literally, "points of view." Usually refers to schools of philosophy.
deva	Benevolent "power." Especially Ṛg Vedic.
dharma	The principle of cosmic, social, and individual order. Also used by the Abhidharma Buddhists to refer to the separate particles of reality.
Dharmakāya	The form of the Buddha as Ultimate Reality.
Dharmaśāstra	Text on the "science of society." The best-known example is by Manu.
dhī	"Vision." Especially Ṛg Vedic.
duḥkha	Painfulness; a description of man's

	experience of *samsāra*. Especially Buddhist.
garbha	Womb or seed.
garbha gṛha	Home of womb or seed. Refers to the inner sanctum of the temple.
Gṛha Sūtra	Text on the "science of household behavior."
guru	Spiritual Teacher.
Indus Valley civilization	A civilization that flourished in the Indus river valley as early as the third millennium B.C. Discovered by archaeologists during this century.
Īśvara	"The Lord." Name of god in manifestation as an object of devotion.
Jainism	Religious movement begun in the sixth century B.C. and still continuing in India today.
jīvanmukta	An Enlightened One who continues to live in this world. Especially Vedāntic.
jñāna	Saving wisdom or divine vision.
Kālī	Cult goddess who combines the attributes of a destroyer with those of a mother. Especially popular in Bengal.
Kali Yuga	The fourth and final age in the world cycle. Marked by a preponderance of evil.
kalpa	A measurement of cosmic time containing many cosmic cycles.
kāma	Pleasure. The third of the four "ends of man."

Kāma Sūtra	Text on the "science of pleasure," especially sexual pleasure.
karma	From the root *kṛ* meaning "to do" or "to work." The word itself means "work." The "law of *karma*" is the understanding that one's works in the present incarnation determine how high or low the next incarnation will be.
karūna	Compassion. Especially in Mahāyāna Buddhism.
Kashmir Śaivism	A school of Śaivism that developed in Kashmir in the late medieval period. It tried to combine Śaivism with Advaita philosophy.
kevala	The Sāṃkhya religious ideal of "separation."
Kṛṣṇa	A popular cultic deity. A form of the god Viṣṇu. Especially popular are stories of his childhood as a mischievous stepson of Yaśodha, and his youth as the flute-playing enchanter of the cowherd girls and lover of Rādha.
Lakṣmī	Goddess of wealth.
līlā	Sport. The nature of the gods' relationship to the world.
liṇga	Symbolic representation of Śiva. Probably phallic.
Madhvā	A medieval theologian who argued a dualist Vedānta.
Mahābalipuram	A small town on the coast south of Madras, containing rock-hewn temples and sculptures from the eighth century.

Mahābhārata	The longest of India's two great epics. Contains the story of the great Bharat war. Probably compiled in the early Christian era.
Manu	A somewhat legendary lawmaker credited with writing the most important Dharmaśāstra text.
māyā	Mysterious veiling power of the world. "Illusion," in the technical language of the Advaita Vedānta.
Mīmāṃsā	A school of philosophy which held that the word (*śabda*) of scripture was the only reality.
mokṣa	Release. The most common Indian word for salvation.
Nāgārjuna	Important Mahayana Buddhist philosopher of the second century.
Naṭarāja	Śiva as "King of the Dance."
nirguṇa	Attribute-less. A description of the highest *Brahman.*
Nirmānakāya	The Buddha when he takes upon himself the changing forms of this world. The Buddha in his human incarnation.
Nirvāna	Non-breath. A name for the highest state of salvation. Especially Buddhist.
Pārvatī	Goddess of the mountains and consort of Śiva.
pāśa	A Śaiva Siddhāntin term for the bonds that keep one in this world.
paśu	A Śaiva Siddhāntin term for the soul conceived of as one of the "cattle" of the Lord.

Pati	A Śaiva Siddhāntin term for Śiva as "Lord" or "Master."
prajñā	Saving wisdom. Especially Buddhist.
prakṛti	"Nature." Particularly in Sāṃkhya-Yoga.
Pṛthvī	The "Earth" personified as a female goddess.
Purāṇa	A class of medieval texts usually described as "mythological histories."
puruṣa	"Man" or "self." Particularly the passive conscious self of Sāṃkhya-Yoga.
puruṣārthas	The "ends" of man; usually the four of *dharma, artha, kāma,* and *mokṣa.*
rāga	The combination of notes that underlies an Indian musical piece.
rajas	"Heat." One of the three aspects of reality in Sāṃkhya-Yoga cosmology.
Rājput	The name of the miniature painting associated with Hindu courts during the Mughal period.
Rāmānuja	Important Vaiṣṇava theologian of the twelfth century.
Rāmāyana	Epic. Contains the story of Rāma and Sīta.
rasa	"Juice." The essence of a work of art which makes it an intimation of that which transcends.
Ṛg Veda	The oldest piece of literature in the Tradition: a collection of Aryan hymns.
ṛṣi	Sage. Especially Ṛg Vedic.

ṛta	Ṛg Vedic concept of cosmic and moral order.
śabda	Word. Important focus in arguments about scriptural authority.
saguṇa	"With attributes." A description of *Brahman* in his manifest forms.
Śaiva Siddhānta	Theistic Śaivism of Southern India.
śakti	"Power." Often pictured as a female aid to the god. Sometimes a separate female deity.
Saṃbhogakāya	The form of the Buddha as a heavenly being: between his forms as manifest in this world and his form as Ultimate Reality.
Saṃhīta	"Collection." Name of early Vedic hymn collections.
Sāṃkhya	Dualist school of philosophy.
samsāra	The "sea of change." Description of life "as it is."
saṃskṛti	"Culture"; that which is refined.
Śaṇkara	Important Advaita Vedānta theologian of the eighth century.
Sarasvatī	Goddess of learning.
śāstra	Scientific treatise.
sat-cit-ānanda	Salvation conceived as a fullness of "being," "consciousness," and "bliss."
satori	Zen Buddhist (Japanese) word for "enlightenment."
sattva	"Light." The highest of the three elements of reality in Sāṃkhya-Yoga cosmology.

Sīta	Goddess and wife of Rāma in the Rāmāyana epic.
Śiva	Important cultic deity.
smṛti	"That which is remembered." Second half of Vedic knowledge.
śruti	"That which is heard." Purest level of Vedic knowledge.
stūpa	Mound-like monument that serves as a center of Buddhist worship.
Śunga	A pre-Christian dynasty famous for its naturalistic art.
Śūnya	"The Void." Nāgārjuna's term for the indescribable Ultimate.
sūtra	"Strand." Treatises made up of short epigrammatic sayings.
svabhāva	"Self-being." A technical philosophical category used by Nāgārjuna.
svadharma	"Self-*dharma.*" The moral order to which an individual feels committed.
tamas	"Heaviness." The lowest of the three elements of reality in Sāṃkhya-Yoga cosmology.
tantra	Sexo-yogic discipline as a religious practice.
Tathāgata	Name of the Buddha as object of devotion.
Theravāda	The "doctrine of the elders." The name of the main school of "southern" Buddhism.
Trikāya	"Three Bodies." The doctrine that the Buddha is manifest in the three

	forms as Ultimate Reality. Heavenly Being, and Earthly Manifestation.
Upaniṣad	Text containing philosophical insights and included in the earliest Vedic collections.
varṇa	"Color." The name of the hierarchical caste system.
veda	"Knowledge." Used to refer to the store of sacred saving knowledge or the "tradition."
vijñāna	Consciousness.
Yakṣi	Feminine tree spirit. Especially in Śunga art.
yoga	"Yoke." Discipline of body, mind, and spirit. School of philosophy.
yogin	One who practices *yoga.*
yuga	A cosmic age.